what
immigrants
hate
about
Canada

What Immigrants Hate About Canada

Now the Lord had said unto Abram, Get thee out of thy country, and from thy kindred, and from thy father's house, unto a land that I will shew thee

The Book of Genesis

This book is dedicated to my wife Naomi, for her love and support. To my parents for bringing me to Canada. And to Mike Harris for angering schoolteachers enough to bring their political opinions into public school classrooms.

Contents

Hate

Hate is a harsh word, an unCanadian word. You're not supposed to say it. You're supposed to say *dislike*. I dislike freezing rain. Canada is full of these *not supposed to's*. You're not even supposed to say *immigrant* anymore, you're supposed to say *newcomer*. So why a book about what immigrants hate about Canada? Because there isn't one written about the subject. Hating America is easy and popular to do, even for Americans, but hating Canada, you're not supposed to.

One in five people in Canada is foreign born: 22% and increasing. Another 18% are second generation immigrants.[1] With so many immigrants we should not only be concerned with growing resentment towards immigrants, but from them as well. This is a largely unheard voice, the hatred that immigrants hold. Hate for other immigrants, politeness, taxes, and even the idea of multiculturalism. You probably never heard that immigrants hate multiculturalism. Well open your mind and remove the stereotypes of a perfect Canada where everyone is nice and polite.

An immigrant is by definition unCanadian, at least at first, until they assimilate into a nice Canadian. What if we don't want to assimilate? We don't have to. That's the idea of multiculturalism, we can keep our culture. What if our culture is rude or homophobic or Islamophobic? Can we keep our hate too? This book will explain the complexities of immigration. Maybe it will help fix some faults in the real Canada, the imperfect Canada.

Canada needs an honest conversation about immigration. Saying 'diversity is our strength' is not good enough. Diversity is complicated. Habitually, concerns about immigration or multiculturalism are rebuffed with accusations of racism. Questions of who, why and how many need to be asked. More importantly these questions must be honestly answered, not just politely placated. With the coronavirus shutdown of 2020-21 tempering migration, perhaps this is a good time to assess immigration and integration in Canada.

Disloyal

What Immigrants Hate about Canada may seem disloyal and ungrateful. We let those immigrants come here and they don't have the decency to show gratitude and patriotism. But it's often ignored how many people born in Canada are disloyal or indifferent to our federation.

In 2004, Newfoundland and Labrador premier Danny Williams ordered Canadian flags to be removed from all provincial buildings. "Why would we fly their flag and pretend everything is rosy?" [2]

Quebec twice held referendums on separation. In 1995 49% of Quebecers voted for independence.[3] Western provinces like Alberta and Saskatchewan feel alienated. In a May 2020 poll, 41% of Albertans surveyed wanted to separate from Canada.[4] Some First Nations bands treat Canada like it's a foreign state. A few Irish Canadians don't want to pledge loyalty to our Queen.[5] Radical Leftists consider Canada imperialist in history, culture and economics.

Many Canadians are not only disloyal to this country, but outright ignorant of it. 75% of Canadians surveyed can't name our Head of State.[6]

There are legions of born Canadians who don't care for, or outright hate Canada. But we expect newcomers to patriotically pledge allegiance. The example set by born Canadians is often apathetic and superficial.

Canada as a foreign country, in Canada. (shutterstock).

Discontent

In truly free and democratic societies you are allowed to hate your country, question your government and burn your flag. Images of American protesters burning their own flag are common and almost a cliché. A cliché that has been upheld by their Supreme Court as free expression.

The Canadian flag has been desecrated on occasion, by Quebec separatists, protesters at the G8 summit, and aboriginal activists.[7] Or at least those claiming to be aboriginal activists. Most Canadians probably don't know that their symbol of peace and tolerance is also burned. And if you told Americans that protesters torch the Canadian flag they would laugh in surprised amusement.

It's mostly leftists and separatists who see Canada as an imperialist state that burn our flag. Some immigrants hate stuff about Canada but it's a much different hate. It's more an annoyance with Canadian pretenses and banalities. Some of our complaints are not really problems with Canada, but inherent difficulties with the process of immigration. Of the newcomers who dislike Canada, most would never come close to desecrating the flag.

Radical Leftists burning the flag in Vancouver. (photo: Stephen Hui)

In the British political tradition, we have the concept of a loyal opposition. Political parties who lost the election, and oppose the government, its laws or policies. The opposition's objective is to criticize with a constructive purpose. Many immigrants feel like an opposition party in our democracy. Unhappy about life in Canada but largely powerless to change the system. This book's purpose is to give a voice to the discontent, with the goal of improving Canada. Many of these issues cannot be easily solved. But changes can be made, the first step is openly and candidly discussing Canadian immigration.

Making another Anne of Green Gables CBC mini-series isn't the only way to improve Canada. *What Immigrants Hate about Canada* may seem controversial, but it's needed. A push to make Canada into the land of opportunity and harmony it's fabled to be.

Kanada

Auschwitz concentration camp was an extermination camp. Prisoners were worked to death, starving along the way. The few that survived usually worked in the *Kanada* section of the camp, spelt with a K in German. This is where luggage from the trains were unloaded. Surrounded by starvation, finding food in the baggage meant this work detail was a relative heaven in the midst of Nazi hell. Hence the nickname Kanada.

For about a hundred years Canada held a special status, a legendary place where everything was perfect. Food and land plentiful, peace and good governance, prosperity and tolerance. Routinely ranked as the best country in the world to live in. Foreigners line up for a chance to enter paradise. And Canada welcomes them, as a nice-polite-tolerant country should.

Then in 2019, this tweet by Shoji Ushiyama:

"As an expat living in Canada, the more I live here, the more I'm convinced I'm actually stuck in some kind of cryptic horror nightmare country that's subtly and slowly eating away at me." [8]

As an immigrant who lived in Canada for 23 years, the "cryptic horror nightmare country eating away at me" was not unexpected. The surprising part is Mr. Ushiyama referred to himself as an expat in Canada. Not a newcomer or an immigrant. Expats are those who study or work in a country and then leave… and return home.

In Canada we have been obsessed with welcoming immigrants and eliminating racism. We made sure Canada loves immigration; you're supposed to. But did we ask the question, do immigrants love Canada?

Expectations

We assume immigrants love Canada because there is no shortage of them. There always seems to be a backlog of applicants, if not 'irregular' migrants crossing from the US border or trying to land a ship on the coast. Part of this is because Canada is a rich Western nation, like the US or Sweden or Germany. Immigrants naturally gravitate towards the stable and prosperous side of the world.

But there's something about Canada, the cherry on top of the west. Canada still has that radiant shine that seduces people, both rich and poor to come to its shores. For poor migrants it's a chance to escape poverty or instability. For affluent newcomers, it's preserving their wealth or another sign of success. The ultimate step on their ladder of accomplishments.

Free health care, a tolerant society, high incomes, good government services, safety and 1st world standards. Immigrants expect a lot from Canada. In many cases immigration consultants are to blame for overselling Canada. But Canada oversells Canada too.

Much of the hate that immigrants have for life in Canada is simply disappointment. This is not the land of milk and honey they were promised. The land they waited years to enter, paid fees, and left their home for. There's something about living in Canada, that slowly eats away at you.

Le Bourgeois Émigré

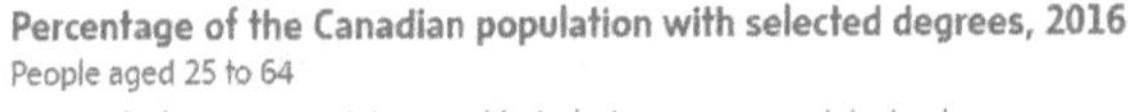

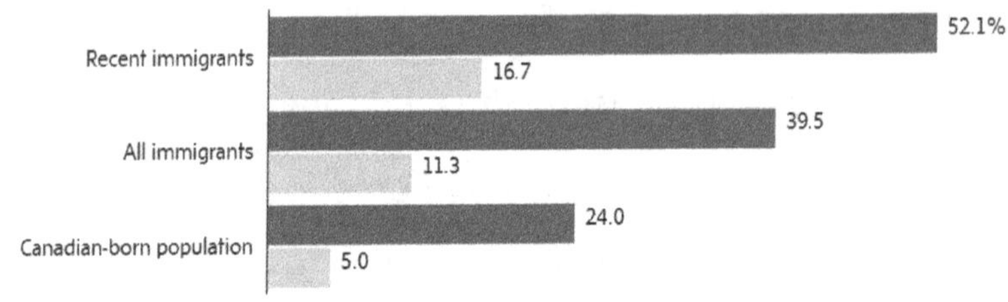

THE GLOBE AND MAIL, SOURCE: STATISTICS CANADA. NOTE: RECENT IMMIGRANTS ARE THOSE WHO FIRST OBTAINED LANDED IMMIGRANT OR PERMANENT RESIDENT STATUS BETWEEN JAN. 1, 2011 AND MAY 10, 2016.

Immigrants more likely to have higher education than born-Canadians

There are old stereotypes of immigrants as poor huddled masses or boat people coming only with the clothes on their backs. However, Canada is blessed by geography. We don't border an unstable Mexico or Middle East. Canada carefully selects its immigrants. As a result, the average modern newcomer isn't poor or underprivileged. You need points to enter Canada. Points and money. We even have business class immigration or investor visa. There are new stereotypes; of rich Chinese,

Ukrainian oligarchs, Dubai jetsetters. The average newcomer is richer, more educated, English speaking and just plain bourgeois.

According to Statistics Canada, half of recent immigrants between the ages of 25 and 64 have a bachelor's degree or higher. These recent immigrants often end up in jobs requiring less than a university education. *Over-education* in Statistics Canada's words.[9]

For many Canada is a step down in their standard of life. Even middle-class immigrants usually feel poorer in Canada. This is largely due to the high cost of living and high cost of labour in Canada. A middle-class Indian with a few extra rupees can afford a cook, a maid to clean the house and a driver to take the kids to school. *Purchasing power* as it's called in economics is a point that needs emphasizing. A middle-class person in a poorer country can have a higher material standard of living than being middle class in a rich country like Canada.

For middle class and above immigrants, life in Canada means you clean your own house and take out your own garbage. And if it's a house in Toronto or Vancouver it's smaller than the one back home. The foreign rich having to clean their own gutter is nothing to cry about, and some Canadians would celebrate this equalization. There is a debate on the economic merit of rich immigrants. They usually bring money into the country, especially when buying a house. The housing issue became a hot topic in Toronto and Vancouver, with local governments adding taxes on foreigners buying homes. Think of it as Canada exporting houses, or Permanent Residence cards.

There is a part of the Canadian government's Immigration and Citizenship's website that reads "Bring as much money as you can."[10] Many newcomers realize that it's their money that is wanted, not their cute cultural diversity. Nevertheless, the result of Canada importing richer folks is they can become disappointed immigrants, angry and resentful.

Much of their cynicism towards Canada reflects the resentment these immigrants receive from Canadians.

Canadians blame them for inflated house prices, for not knowing *their place* as immigrants, and are suspect of the source of their wealth. There's something about a rich person from a poor country that doesn't sit well with middle class Westerners.

The third world isn't what it used to be, thanks to economic growth and globalization. Immigrants leave behind good jobs, businesses, family, friends and servants for a life in Canada that can leave them bitter and cold.

How much money you should bring

Research how much it costs to live in the place where you plan to settle in Canada.

Bring as much money as you can. This will make moving and finding a home in Canada easier. When you arrive in Canada, you have to tell the border officer if you're bringing

Poor immigrants

Poor people tend to be less disappointed in coming to Canada, usually because their opportunity cost is low. What they left behind wasn't much, at least in material terms. Coming to the Promised Land is still a big risk, a roll of the dice that may or may not work out. The hard part is if it doesn't work out, they don't have anything to fall back on.

The difficulty starts with the application process. Details on your five siblings, then details on your wife's seven siblings. Medical exams. Police background checks and bank statements. Borrow money and pretend to be rich before printing the bank statements. Sending documents, then waiting, paying fees, and more waiting.

In the event you do get accepted into Canada, there are new problems. Much of what you were promised disappears like a mirage. Some are told by overseas immigration consultants that there's free food in Canada. Only to find out they're referring to food banks.

Many poor immigrants in Canada were middle-class professionals in their home country. They naively assumed they could continue being doctors or lawyers once in Canada. You could of course, after some expensive and time-consuming schooling to upgrade your foreign credentials. For now they're doing whatever low paid jobs they could get.

A few decades ago anyone could get a basic job, own a small home in Scarborough and live comfortably. With the cost of living, especially housing so high, those days are over. The Canadian system is designed to serve middle class Westerners, not poor people.

In poor countries governments try to ensure food and fuel are inexpensive for consumers. In Canada, we have supply management, which increases the cost of basics like milk. Not to mention multiple layers of gas taxes. In poor countries governments sometimes give away land and home building supplies, or at least subsidize the cost. In Canada, we have the Ontario greenbelt that reduces the supply of developable land. And lots of building and zoning regulations. All of them necessary of course. For newcomers in the Toronto or Vancouver area, don't bother trying to explain why a small house costs $900,000. It would only further destroy their dreams.

It may make sense for affluent overseas folk to cash in their chips and move to Canada. Highly skilled and educated immigrants still have a good chance of living the Canadian dream, even if resentfully. But for low skilled immigrants without much money, things are different. New unskilled immigrants typically get low paid jobs to start their career ladder and work their way up. But the unfortunate reality of high minimum wage regulations is it prices some low skilled immigrants out of work.[11] The system is set up to make the middle class *feel* like they live in a *just society*, rather than help the poor.

Kathy Katula, protesting high electricity costs. $1200 monthly Hydro bill. (photo: The Peterborough Examiner, Skarstedt)

Middle class Politics

You're not supposed to say *poor people*, you're supposed to say "those working hard to enter the middle class". From English to Canadian English those two words become eight. There will be another chapter for political correctness. But here we will focus on the middle class, it's the Canadian thing to do.

Newcomers are usually confused as to who or what is this middle class they keep hearing about. Especially around election season everyone is talking about the middle class. It sounds good, you're supposed to be it.

In 2019 Prime Minister Justin Trudeau appointed a Minister of Middle Class Prosperity. Asked to define the middle class, Trudeau said "Canadians know who's in the middle class and know what their families are facing and we focus more on the actual issues". Minister of Middle Class Prosperity Mona Fortier was able to clarify: "I define the middle class where people feel that they can afford their way of life... They have quality of life. And they can ... send their kids to play hockey or even have different activities." [12]

That does sound good. Poor people, immigrants and born Canadians alike get irritated at this unrelenting focus on people who are doing just fine. Not only is there no emphasis on helping the actual poor, but middle class policies usually end up hurting the poor.

Labour regulations that incentivize companies to *not* hire workers. Land regulations to make housing scarce. Life in Canada is becoming more unaffordable for the poor because laws and regulations are made by the middle class for the middle class, who can "afford their way of life".

Other immigrants

In the 2006 *Borat* film, Borat a Kazakh visitor to the US passes the Uzbek embassy and shouts insults at his rival country.[13] While most academics, activists and journalists focus on hate and racism originating from white people, a lot of hate is immigrant on immigrant hate. This is not simple humour about Trinidad versus Guyana or Kazakhstan versus Uzbekistan.

The world is charged with centuries of brutal history between peoples, states and religions. We bring them to Canada and expect them to sing John Lennon's *Imagine* as they exit the plane. Unfortunately, the hate comes with them. A currently popular myth among academics and activists is that racism is dependent on a white power hierarchy. This is dehumanizing as it assumes only white people are capable of racism. Immigrants are human too and have deep seated racism to prove it.

Most newcomers didn't grow up in politically correct cultures where they learnt about the horrors of the holocaust. They come from countries where stereotyping is a way of life and *Mein Kampf* is still a bestseller. In 2005 over 100,000 copies of Hitler's book were sold in Turkey, in only two months.[14]

Immigrants don't just hate immigrants from other countries, in many cases they hate their own countrymen. The comedian Russell Peters once explained the difference between a terrorist and an Indian. Terrorists hate America, Indians hate each other.[15]

Indians from south India resent the many north Indians in Canada. The north is "the most backward part of India". Needless to say what Indians think of the two hundred thousand Pakistanis in Canada. Hong Kong Chinese feel overshadowed by the large, growing and less refined mainland Chinese population. Then there are the Arabs, everyone loves the Arabs. Since Black people have been in North America for centuries, many think of themselves as the default and resident minority group. They see other minorities as foreigners. Especially the "greedy" Indians and Chinese. And most of these foreign newcomers will soon judge Black people by what they see on the evening news.

Lazy Romanians hate the arrogant Poles, and the Poles hate the malevolent Russians. There is a gordian knot of hate and distrust between the many ethnic groups that make up the Canadian mosaic. Immigrants expect to see white people in Canada but are sometimes shocked at the amount of other people here too. The shock becomes disgust when the other people are from countries and cultures they don't like.

The complicated relationship among immigrants play out in many aspects of Canadian life, such as the jobs market. As Statistics Canada cited, "the competitive effects of additional immigrant inflows are concentrated among immigrants themselves."[16]

If you asked immigrants if they support more immigration, the honest response would be *immigration from where exactly?*

Montreal Armenian protestor against the Azeri/Turkish side (photo: Margossian / The Link)

Racism

Everyone knows America is an evil racist country full of white supremists, but Canada is open, polite, and tolerant remember? As Mathew Amha notes in Maclean's, we have a "national story of a nation whose history is perched atop a summit of myth and fiction."

Racism in Canada is usually viewed through the lens of anti-Americanism. Amha writes "It's a historical assessment that distances Canada from responsibility and complicity in the franchise of racism. It has recreated the country in the vision of a kind of apologia—that we were bad, but not as bad as *them*. Sure we're a little racist, but *they are worse*."

Canada's history of slavery is largely unknown, especially cases where slaves escaped *from Canada* into free states in America. [17]

Even in modern times, there exists Canadian racism that lurks below the surface. Implied racism that you know is there but can't be fully seen. This isn't some guy in a pickup truck racism. It comes from officialdom at times and places you least expect.

Examples include former Mississauga mayor Hazel McCallion, quoted in the National Post saying hospitals' "emergency is loaded with people in their native costumes"[18]. McCallion says it was out of context. Or Hockey Night in Canada's Don Cherry's Remembrance Day lament "You people that come here... you love our way of life, you love our milk and honey, at least you can pay a couple bucks for a poppy or something like that..."[19]

The problem for most immigrants isn't that this is hurtful. It is mostly confusing. What symbols or dress would be seen as a native costume? What else do I have to do to be accepted as a normal Canadian and not be "you people". Because of the façade of multiculturalism, it isn't clear how to fit in, or whether fitting in would solve the problem at all.

Multiculturalism

Former British Prime Minister David Cameron said, "state multiculturalism is a wrong-headed doctrine that has had disastrous results." German Chancellor Angela Merkel: "this [multicultural] approach has failed, utterly failed." The United States avoided multiculturalism, with its melting pot where immigrants are supposed to become American.

Multiculturalism is a policy where different cultures can maintain their culture and identities while collaborating with each other. Canada has pioneered and maintained state multiculturalism. Firstly, to differentiate from the American model. Secondly, to reassure French Canada (mostly Quebec) that their status and culture would be preserved and celebrated. Many in Quebec were in fact reassured under the then new policy of multiculturalism.

However, the theory doesn't work well in practice. Europe has learnt the lesson and Australia is currently being schooled. Ironically, Quebec is now leading the charge against multiculturalism, after seeing the effects of this policy. There will be a separate chapter on Quebec. But here we will remind foreign readers that Quebec now has laws that require residents to remove cultural or religious face coverings when receiving public services. There is another law to prevent certain government employees from wearing religious symbols.

Multiculturalism has another critic in Canada, immigrants. Newcomers have become the face of this policy, so it's a tough pill to swallow that many immigrants hate the cult of multiculturalism in Canada. It's actually the title of an award-winning book: *Selling Illusions: The Cult of Multiculturalism in Canada*, by Neil Bissoondath.[20] You probably never heard of this book, you're not supposed to. Bissoondath is not only an immigrant, but also a fellow native of Trinidad.

Bissoondath argues that multiculturalism discourages full loyalty to Canada and turns historical distinctions into stereotyped commodities. Seeing people celebrating your *native costumes* can be just as patronizing as criticizing your native costumes. To paraphrase George Orwell, I know enough about other cultures to not idealize them.

Many immigrants hate multiculturalism because it allows other immigrants to keep their culture as well. As stated earlier, immigrants hold many prejudices against other newcomers. This is especially true for immigrants who have been here for decades. They have paid their dues to Canada and think new migrants are getting a free ride. Or worse, bringing inferior lifestyles and habits to Canada.

Communities holding on to foreign culture can be a burden for some. Individuals can feel imprisoned by a surrounding ethnic culture that refuses to change. This can be especially true for women from more traditional cultures.

Another problem newcomers have with multiculturalism is its ambiguity. What part of my culture can I keep? Can I have two wives? Can I spit on the sidewalk? What if my culture isn't as liberal as Canadian society would like? It usually isn't. Some immigrants end up living double lives, modern Westerners in public and traditional Afghans in private. To some, the true definition of multiculturalism is you can keep the parts of your culture that are acceptable to white people. Surveys now show that Canadians are much less keen of multiculturalism than officially proclaimed. According to an Angus Reid poll, 68% think minorities should do more to fit in with mainstream culture. [21]

On Diversity

 Minorities should do more to fit in with mainstream American/Canadian society

 We should encourage cultural diversity with different groups keeping their own customs and languages

CANADA

68% | 32%

UNITED STATES

53% | 47%

Canadians less multicultural than America? (photo: Angus Reid/CBC News).

First Nations

Broad cultural grouping of North American Indigenous peoples, the continent sometimes called Turtle Island

In other countries we are taught that everything is perfect in Canada. The consultants and agents selling immigration insist on this. Upon arrival we hear that *reconciliation* is needed in Canada. A word commonly used for South Africa's way of dealing with apartheid. There are frequent protests by aboriginals and those acting in their name. Occasionally these become blockades of roads and rail, impeding life for everyone else. The government is seemingly always apologizing for past crimes against the native peoples.

The status of First Nations in Canada is confusing to newcomers. Most everything is named after the indigenous peoples. They get spotlight performances for the opening of the Olympic or PanAm games. And above all, they lived all their lives in Canada, the best country in the world. What can possibly be wrong? Apparently, a lot, judging by the constant protests and government apologies.

From the early days of European settlement, the native peoples of Canada have suffered colonial oppression. Up until recent decades children were taken from their families, placed in residential schools, to be forcibly assimilated into white Canadian culture. Many suffering additional abuse beyond the loss of family, language and culture. In 2015, the Truth and Reconciliation Commission of Canada found that this amounted to cultural genocide.[22] Cultural genocide? That wasn't in the *come to the best country in the world* brochure.

This history isn't always known to newcomers who didn't go through the Canadian education system. More often, what is known is that natives get special treatment. Seeing someone not pay taxes in Walmart can be an eyebrow raising moment for a new immigrant scraping by. Then we hear rumors of the government money they get. And corporate money from mining and oil companies operating on their land. Knowledge gained by envy is more lavish than knowledge gained by sympathy.

There is a sense among immigrants that Canada is always paying a debt to the aboriginals. And that debt will never be fully paid. Many newcomers view first nations with the skepticism common among born Canadians.

There is a perception that first nations get special treatment. And newcomers silently ask: why? Is it because they were here first? Where does that place immigrants on the pecking order? Newcomers, by definition, arrived last. Is it because they were wronged and abused by imperialism? Most immigrants are also descendants of colonialism and slavery, and some survivors of actual genocide. Many of our foreign ancestors were wronged by the same British Crown that victimized North American natives. Doesn't the Crown owe us reconciliation too?

Canadians (including new Canadians) sometimes use immigration to insinuate that aboriginals just don't help themselves. If new immigrants can do well in Canada, why can't someone who has been here forever? This of course ignores that immigration is an entrepreneurial endeavor. And that Canada is biased towards selecting richer and more educated newcomers.

Even if first nations get special treatment, that special treatment seems to do no good. Probably because the special treatment is purely symbolic. Virtue signalling as it's sometimes called. African-American Economist Thomas Sowell, who spent decades researching race and culture, states that there is an inverse relationship between political activism and economic success.[23] Native political protests result in political appeasement, which is ultimately worthless.

In 2017 Prime Minister Trudeau said, "No relationship is more important to Canada than the relationship with Indigenous Peoples". That's good appeasement, while delivering nothing practical. At least it clarifies the pecking order in society. Trudeau's government is also planning on changing the oath of citizenship to highlight aboriginal rights.

Proposed text of oath of citizenship:

"I swear (or affirm) that I will be faithful & bear true allegiance to Her Majesty Queen Elizabeth the Second, Queen of Canada, Her Heirs & Successors, & that I will faithfully observe the laws of Canada, ___including the Constitution, which recognizes and affirms the___

<u>***Aboriginal & treaty rights of First Nations, Inuit & Métis***</u> <u>***peoples***</u>*, & fulfil my duties as a Canadian citizen."*[24]

Now new Canadians can join the government in paying lip service to first nations.

Most First Nations communities would prefer to have practical governance instead of virtuous words. If a small percentage of the symbolic niceties and land acknowledgements translated into jobs or education or clean water, this chapter wouldn't be necessary. Unfortunately, many indigenous Canadians live in third world conditions with little hope of improvement. This, in the best country in the world to live in.

this book isn't the first un-Canadian book

The Best Country in the World

Everyone will tell you that Canada is the best country in the world to live in. It's not just their opinion, it's published in international rankings. Canadian media will never let you miss it. Our annual self-congratulation when Canada is ranked number one in the world. Either overall or 'quality of life' or some other swimsuit category. Some unfortunate years we place second behind the undeserving Australia or Norway.

The US News & World Report's 2020 rankings placed Canada second overall, behind Switzerland. But the index that started this fad was the HDI. The Human Development Index was started in 1990 by the United Nations Development Programme. The goal was to measure countries' development in more a comprehensive approach instead of just Gross Domestic Product (GDP). Health and education were the new metrics considered, along with income.

For much of the 1990's Canada was ranked top in the list. Along with hockey, self-congratulating became another national past time. Immigrants would keep reminding themselves that they now live in the best country in the world. Chronic problems, such as indigenous living standards would be chronically ignored. The delivery of health care didn't need reforming, just reassuring that it was 'free' and best in the world.

Canadians forgot or overlooked that the HDI was not designed for countries like Canada or Switzerland. It was intended for Bolivia and Botswana. Comparing the literacy rate of Norway to Sweden is largely pointless. 99.12% vs 99.13%. Most rich Western countries cluster at the top with little difference in rankings. The statistical calculation method used has more influence than any meaningful differences. Reporting the HDI of the top 15 countries adds no value other than fodder for the second half of the evening news.

The HDI was not meant for Westerners to feel good about their place in the world. It was meant to measure and advise nations struggling with development. If Bangladesh is moving up the rankings, while Pakistan is not, now we could investigate. Policies and laws could be adjusted. Lessons learned could be applied to other countries facing similar challenges.

The HDI is a useful tool for the developing world where starvation and female bondage is common. It is of no value for Canadians, other than to stroke our ego and ignore our problems.

There are now additional indices, such as the US News & World Report. The focus is still at the top of the list, like a Miss Universe competition. A successful and self-assured nation would ignore these rankings, or at least try to learn lessons from development overseas. But Canada is not confident. We concentrate and elaborate on every superficial beauty contest where we win. Or at least place higher than America.

TABLE 2.10
HDI ranking for industrial 1994

Country	HDI value	HDI rank
Canada	0.960	1
France	· 0.946	2
Norway	0.943	3
USA	0.942	4
Iceland	0.942	5

TABLE 1.8
HDI ranking for industri 1993

Country	HDI value	HDI rank
Canada	0.951	1
USA	0.940	2
Japan	0.938	3
Netherlands	0.938	4
Norway	0.937	5

TABLE 2

HDI ranks, 1998

1 Canada
2 Norway
3 United States
4 Australia
5 Iceland

Better-than-America-stan

The country formerly known as Canada.

There is an obsession with the United States in Canada and being better than it. Morally superior, intellectually superior, virtuous. We thank God, we are not like those Americans; extortioners, unjust, adulterers.

Especially that Donald Trump, such a bad guy. Trump is so vile he prefers the Canadian immigration system and would like to implement it in the US.[25] This is another point that must be repeated to the majority of Canadians who will gloss over that line. The evil-right-wing-racist-Islamophobe-xenophobe-nativist-republican loves the Canadian immigration system.

Yet we continue to believe that Canadian immigration is virtuous and humanitarian. We're supposed to. Canadian multiculturalism is better than the American melting pot. It must be, it's Canadian.

Our McDonald's logo has a small maple leaf in it. See how vastly different we are. Most immigrants consider Canada and the US to be very similar nations. Americans also think Canada is *America Junior* or the 51st state. But Canadians see a vast gulf of righteousness that separates us from those Philistines. Politicians will accuse each other of using American style ads or for working in the US. Corporations, some with headquarters south of the border, will market to us by stroking our ego about the *Canadian way*. The implication is always, Canada is better than America.

Newcomers from small countries that are next to big countries will recognize this. It's an inferiority complex that masquerades as a superiority complex.

It's ignored that about one million Canadians choose to live in the US. Better weather, higher incomes, lower taxes, lower cost of living, more variety of places to live, and more diversity.

Yes, America has more cultural diversity than Canada. Canada is about 73% white. The US is also 73% white, but that falls to 61% if you only count non-Hispanic whites.[26] Furthermore, most of Canada's whites are concentrated in British and French heritage. American whites better represent other European nations, with larger percentages of Germans, Jews, and lots of Hispanic whites.

Then there is the brain drain. With a larger economy and more capitalism to exploit, Canada's top talent moves south. Not only A-list celebrities, even doctors and engineers can double their incomes by leaving Canada. It doesn't matter how much our singer-songwriters represent Canada. They're cashing their cheques in Atlanta and Las Vegas.

Now we know why Canada needs highly skilled immigrants. To replace our brain drained emigrants. The inferiority complex also explains Canada's obsession with immigration. A constant stream of foreign applicants eager to enter Canada reassures us that Canada is great too.

Canadian pop culture is almost-American, but also anti-American

Muslims

This chapter deals with the hate towards as well as from Muslim immigrants. As mentioned earlier, some immigrants hate other newcomers, Muslims included.

In 2017 the Canadian parliament passed a non-binding motion to condemn Islamophobia in Canada. Many immigrants believed this was another example of *them* getting special treatment. Islamophobia is usually defined as hate or fear of Muslims or Islam.

A 2016 FORUM poll suggested 28% of Canadians had an unfavourable view of Muslims.[27] Most would assume this prejudice is white prejudice. However most white Canadians' fear of Muslims started with the September 11th, 2001 attacks. Before this date there was little media coverage or information on Islam in Canada. In the rest of the world other nations had relations with Muslims that go back centuries. Good and bad relations, but in this book we will focus on the bad. This is where the hate comes from.

In southeastern Europe, Islam is associated with Ottoman Turkish colonialism. The Ottomans ruled the Balkans for centuries, with invasions, slavery and all the tragedy of imperialism. Even today, many eastern European immigrants cannot separate the word Muslim from the historical Ottoman connotations.

In India, Islamophobia probably started in the late 7th century. Invasions by Muhammad bin Qasim, Timur and Nader Shah are still fresh in the minds of many Indians, centuries after. In the Greater Toronto Area, some Hindu immigrants have tried to keep 'religious accommodation' out of schools, protesting against Islamic prayers in schools.[28]

Much of Western China is populated by east Turkic Muslims commonly known as Uyghurs. China has reportedly imprisoned up to a million of these Muslims in re-education camps.[29] The objective lying somewhere between assimilation and de-Islamization. Such is the fear of Islam among other nations.

That fear comes to Canada by way of immigration. A major object of hate for newcomers in Canada is Muslim immigration. Many immigrants believe there are too many Muslims in Canada. They are also thought to receive special treatment in this country. The parliamentary motion to condemn islamophobia and the Prime Ministerial welcome for Syrian refugees are seen as prime examples. Even though there were earlier parliamentary motions to condemn discrimination against Jews and Yazidis, and many of the Syrian refugees were Christian.

In 2020, cities across Canada allowed mosques to broadcast the Islamic call to prayer during Ramadan on loudspeakers. This quickly became an example to some that Muslims get special treatment.

Muslims are not only the victims of hate, but the source of some of it. A few Muslims have been arrested for plotting terror attacks against Canadian targets. In 2006, eighteen young Muslims were arrested for planning attacks against the Canadian Broadcasting Corporation

(CBC) and Parliament. From the Greater Toronto Area, some were born in Canada of immigrant parents and others arrived when they were kids.[30] Their hatred for Canada is probably just the hatred for Western nations that radical Islamist extremists usually embody. This hate may be generic anti-America, anti-West, but it is extreme and violent.

On the more normal end of the spectrum, some Muslim immigrants prefer an Islamic society. Many don't want their children raised in an excessively progressive Canada. In 2015, the Liberal Ontario government introduced changes to the sexual education curriculum. Muslims reacted instantly, alarmed at gender identity and sexual orientation being taught too early, if at all. Muslims protested and kept their children home from school on some days. At Thorncliffe Park Elementary, which is largely Muslim, only 130 out of 1,350 students attended school one day.[31]

Muslims choosing to leave Islamic countries and complain that Canada is not Islamic may seem confusing.

But this is the complex nature of immigration that cannot be sugar coated with clichés of "diversity is our strength."

While some believe Muslims get special treatment in Canada, some Muslims feel the complete opposite.

Due to conflicts in the Middle East, many Muslims come to Canada with a pre-existing sense of victimhood and persecution. Incidents in Canada can add to a feeling that this country is also against them. Mosques are sometimes vandalized. Rumors of Hijabs being ripped off. The government wanting to set up a hotline for *barbaric cultural practices*. According to one survey, 30% of Muslim Canadians say they have experienced discrimination. The same survey found more Muslims were 'very proud' to be Canadian (83%) than non-Muslim Canadians (73%). Their greatest source of pride reported is Canada's freedom and democracy.[32]

High profile events can deeply affect perceptions. In 2017 six were killed and nineteen injured in a shooting at a mosque in Quebec City. Unfortunately, many Muslim immigrants were not surprised by this violent action. The white nationalist perpetrator was seen only as an extreme example of prejudice against Muslims in Canada.

Furthermore, as the Meadowvale Islamic Centre demonstrated (see image), the difficulty in getting a mosque approved and built shows the true face of diversity and multiculturalism in Canada.

While proud to be Canadian, Muslim newcomers who believed the promises of freedom of worship, tolerance and openness can be left with a feeling that life in Canada is just as discriminatory as in Tajikistan. Just much more expensive.

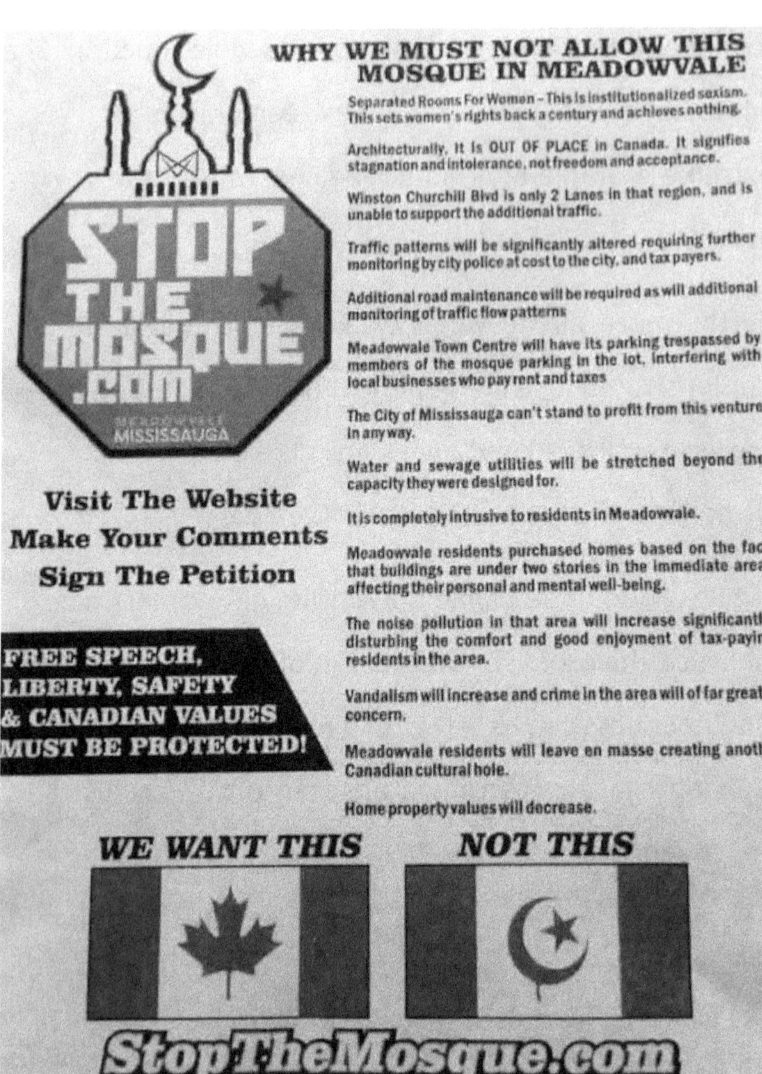

Poster against the Meadowvale Islamic Centre (Mississauga, Ontario)

Quebec

In 2005 Tajikistan banned female students from wearing Islamic headscarves in secular schools. The education minister explained that the hijab "is unacceptable in secular schools and violates the constitution and a new law on education."[33] Tajikistan is mostly Muslim, with a state that strives towards secularism.

In 2019, Quebec banned public officials in positions of authority from wearing religious symbols. Affected officials include teachers, police, and judges. Residents are also required to uncover their faces when receiving public services. Everyone assumes this is designed to keep the Muslim hijab and niqab out of Quebec's public life.[34]

Then there are the language laws. Signs in French must be "markedly predominant" and have a "greater visual impact" than signs in any other language.[35] An 'other language' is commonly used to refer to English. The Office Québécois de la Langue Française (Quebec Board of the French Language) gained a reputation for citing businesses, hospitals and small towns for using only English or not enough French. One famous example was an Italian restaurant cited for using the word *Pasta* on its menu.

Quebec's overzealous protection of their language and secularism is imposing and confusing to immigrants. It's also seemingly vindictive if you're a Muslim immigrant. Most newcomers are not familiar with its history and where the zeal comes from.

After the British conquered Canada, French Canadians soon found themselves subjugated. In eastern Canada French Acadians were deported with many dying along the way. And in Quebec, the French were now an oppressed majority. The English would come to dominate the business world while the French would form a lower class of workers and peasants. Some English aristocrats treated the French as non-white subjects. Being told to 'speak white' (English) instead of French, this discrimination entered the lore of Quebecois sentiments. For many the Catholic church was a haven for French culture, and would come to dominate politics in the province until the 1960's.

Then came the Quiet Revolution, turning conservative Catholic Quebec into staunchly secular and borderline socialist. The French would soon consolidate political power, even holding referendums to separate from Canada. In the 1995 referendum a tight 50.58% of Quebec voted to remain in Canada.

The vote was close with most French speaking Quebecois voting *Yes,* in favour of sovereignty. The *No* vote won largely due to English speakers in the province. Separatist Premier Jacques Parizeau, disappointed and speaking after the close result, blamed "money and the ethnic vote."[36]

Early immigrants in Quebec, mostly Italians, Greeks, Jews, aligned with the downtrodden French against the arrogant English. Now that the French were in power, the *ethnic vote* sided with English speakers.

Immigrants in Quebec mostly voted with English speakers to remain in Canada. Loyalty to Canada was one reason. Another key reason was the fear of Quebecois ethnonationalism.

People who were oppressed find it difficult to understand their oppression of others. Immigrants in Quebec knew they could one day call themselves *Canadian*, but not *Quebecois*, an ethnic term. Terms such as *Pur Laine* (pure wool) and *de souche* (the base of the tree), are other words that imply old stock white French Quebecois are the true people of Quebec.

Newcomers in Quebec feel more foreign and excluded than newcomers in the rest of Canada. In 2006, author Jan Wong controversially alleged that Quebec society is concerned with racial purity.[37]

Ethnocentrism, language police, restrictions on religious symbols. Quebec in many ways reminds us of Tajikistan, Turkey or wherever we came from.

NATIONAL ASSEMBLY OF QUÉBEC

FIRST SESSION   FORTY-SECOND LEGISLATURE

Bill 21

An Act respecting the laicity of the State

Free Health Care

Free health care in the best country in the world. Who wouldn't migrate for that? The sparkle comes off Canada after you actually need health care and end up in the emergency room. After seven hours of waiting in the emergency room, waiting room, and then actual room, now you know the cost of *free* health care.

In Ontario, *hallway medicine* became a common term for patients in more spacious rooms. Also known as hospital hallways since actual rooms were full. If you need surgery or a procedure, you better have a good book to read for the next few months as you wait.

According to the Fraser Institute (2020), of 28 developed countries Canada spends the 2nd highest on health care but ranks near the bottom for the number of doctors, hospital beds, and wait times.[38]

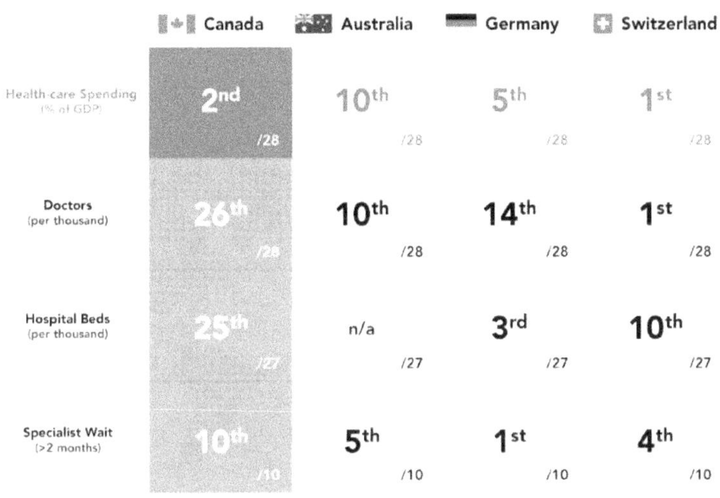

Many Canadians tolerate the long wait, rushed doctors, and hallway medicine because it's supposedly free and egalitarian. Winston Churchill called socialism the equal sharing of misery. Welcome to Canada Winston.

Except it isn't egalitarian. Rich Canadians simply visit a hospital in the United States, Thailand or India for fast and sophisticated service. Canadian politicians who must pledge allegiance to universal health care and resolutely oppose 'two-tier health care' usually try to keep their American medical visits below the radar. This Includes former Prime Minister Jean Chretien and former Premiers Robert Bourassa and Danny Williams.[39] At least they pay lip service to universal pretenses.

In 2005, Supreme Court of Canada Chief Justice McLachlin wrote "Access to a waiting list is not access to health care."[40] Many newcomers find that out the painful way. When it's tax paying time immigrants also realize the true cost of 'free' health care.

Newcomers who were middle class and above in their home countries are accustomed to getting immediate health care. Other countries are less ideological when it comes to health, you can buy it with money when you need it. In Canada, that is the forbidden, illegal, greedy, capitalist two-tier health care system. Bringing newcomers who are used to buying health care when needed to Canada, where it is delivered when available is a recipe for unhappy immigrants.

Immigrants never forget that passing medical tests was part of the immigration process. You must be reasonably healthy to be allowed here in the first place. Immigrants are deemed 'medically inadmissible' if they would be a danger to public health or place excessive demand on health and social services.[41] Canada wants healthy newcomers. Don't add to the shared misery.

Stockwell Day obeying Canadian doctrine, during the 2000 Federal election (CP photo).

Education

According to the 2016 Statistics Canada census, two out of five children in Canada are either immigrants or have an immigrant parent.[42]

For most immigrants, education is valued at a level that few old stock Canadians can understand. Most of us come from countries that were desperately poor a few decades ago. Our parents sometimes couldn't dream of a better life for themselves but were comforted in the hope that their children would succeed. Children's education was everything. A better life for the next generation. The leveller in an unequal world. Parent's pension plan.

Canadian schools are irritating to many newcomers. Almost every ethnicity hates the school system for a different reason.

The Toronto District School Board (TDSB) studied the high school cohort between 2006 and 2011. The results were hard hitting.

Variable	Subgroup	Total	Graduated	Still in TDSB	Drop-out (no information)
Racial Group	White	4,854	81.9%	6.1%	12.0%
	East Asian	2,778	91.1%	2.6%	6.3%
	South Asian	2,773	87.0%	3.0%	10.0%
	Black	1,718	64.5%	12.7%	22.8%
	Mixed	825	73.0%	8.7%	18.3%
	Middle Eastern	666	77.5%	6.5%	16.1%
	South East Asian	536	84.1%	7.1%	8.8%
	Latin	292	69.9%	9.6%	20.5%

TDSB grade 9 cohort 2006-2011

Only 65% and 70% of Black and Latin students graduated. A stark contrast against 91% and 87% of East Asian and South Asians. White students were in the middle at 82%.[43]

For Black parents, education in Canada is depressing. High drop out rates. Students 'pushed out' of schools. Young people were streamed away from university or college. In 2006-07 Black students were three times more likely to be suspended than white students.[44]

In our home countries, students are taught to respect authority and often fear their teachers. In Canada, authority is a bad word, students must be free to find themselves. The lack of authority and order in Canadian schools is probably the main reason Black students fall through the cracks. It is certainly not the difficulty of the curriculum. Some critics point out that cultural baggage keeps Black and Latin youth down. In multicultural Canada you're not supposed to blame culture for anything, so it's therefore the fault of the Canadian school system.

Some say the curriculum is Eurocentric or lacks ethnic influence. This clearly doesn't hinder East Asian and South Asian kids who routinely outperform white students. Many Asian parents hate the schools for being too easy and focused on soft sciences. You can't boast to other Asian parents about how well your kids are doing, since anyone who actually attends school does well. The lack of authority is unknown to some parents, who can't imagine a school without order.

The 2020 coronavirus pandemic was eye-opening to many immigrant parents. Online at-home schooling became common in many provinces. For the first time parents saw the lack of academic rigour and excessive emphasis on social skills at Canadian schools.

Politicized teachers who are often on strike is another pain for newcomers. Each student generation remembers teachers railing in front of the class against Mike Harris, Dalton McGuinty, Kathleen Wynn and Doug Ford. A noble Ontario tradition. Apparently, every Premier from either party is intent on destroying education, crushing teacher's rights and impoverishing students.

Higher Education

the unofficial logo of Ryerson University painted on the sidewalk

Walk through some Canadian universities and posters for 'Socialist Action' and 'Marxist Syndicalism' will brighten your day. Trotskyists meeting at the pub will remind you of the good old days, 1920's Moscow. Many immigrants come from formally communist countries, such as China and Vietnam. After tasting economic growth, these countries have reformed to a point where some students see more socialism in Canadian university than in the People's Republic.

Most immigrants ignore the excessive politics on campus and focus on academics. According to Maclean's magazine (2010), at the University of British Columbia 40% of students are Asian and none of them were on the student executive.[45]

Focusing on academic success is not a casual choice for many of immigrant background. Education is a primal unrelenting necessity for those of Asian and African cultures. TV's Nigerian Abishola forcing her son toward medical school is more reality than comedy.[46] Large numbers of especially Asian and South Asian newcomers have created a culture clash among students.

As Maclean's declared "that Asian students work harder is a fact born out by hard data."

"White students, by contrast, are more likely to choose universities and build their school lives around social interaction, athletics and self-actualization—and, yes, alcohol. When the two styles collide, the result is separation rather than integration."

Social interaction and Self-actualization is white people talk for wasting time, dicking around, drinking and partying. Finding yourself.

Asians who are focused on academics are regarded as nerds and resented for taking the spots of white kids. White students must work harder and party less to compete with Asians. The fun college culture is changing. Many American universities are restricting Asian student numbers, ironically in the name of diversity.

Asians resent being placed in the violin playing nerd category. They hate the fact Canadian universities are built around alcohol, self-indulgence, and leftist politics. In academia, it seems that academically minded students are the odd ones out.

Immigrants feel marginalized in university. Not just overachieving Asians. Muslims who don't drink alcohol, and those who are somehow, politically conservative.

International Students

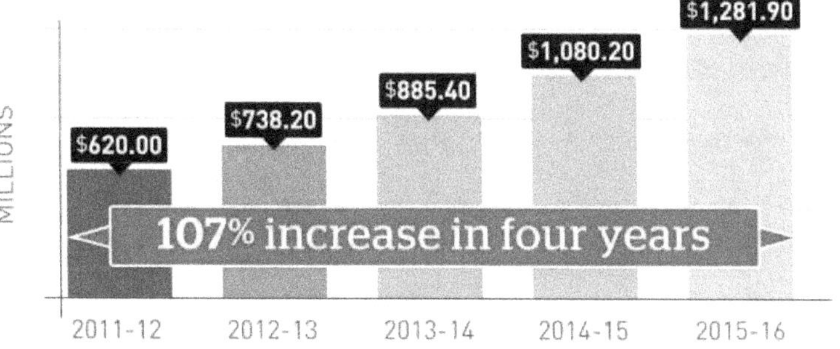

According to Statistics Canada, the average undergraduate university tuition fee for the 2019/2020 year is $6,468. The average for international undergrads in Canada is $29,883. In Ontario, the average fee is $7,931 for Canadians and $38,108 for international students.[47]

Why does it cost four times as much to educate an international student? One reason for the large price gap is because university is heavily subsidized for Canadians. It is subsidized by governments and by foreigners.

Foreign students and their money are being used to finance Canadian students and bloated university administrations.

Foreigners are willing to pay for a brand name Western degree. Canadian universities are more than willing to charge them like a Mercedes-Benz dealership.

Another example of the Canadian business model also known as immigration. According to some reports, international students contribute more to university revenue than government funding.

There are over half a million study-visa holders in Canada. Not all international students are children of the foreign rich. Some families see this as an alternative route to permanent residence and citizenship. According to the Vancouver Sun (2019) some parents sell off their assets to get their children to Canada. Others go into debt. Once here, the students are open to exploitation. They know what their families sacrificed for a chance at immigration. Some work more than the permitted 20 hours per week. Some are exploited and sexually harassed, living in fear of being reported or deported. Students take on debt of their own to pay fees and others end up working in the drug trade.[48]

The Globe and Mail reported some international students are paying large sums to get jobs as truck drivers. Having a job can help them get qualified for permanent residency. Working past their 20-hour limit, they can be arrested and deported.[49]

International students are often not counted as part of immigration. They are seen as education tourists bringing money and supporting university budgets. Not all are children of oligarchs and government officials. Many are ordinary immigrants by another name, through another route. Overseas agents sell them the usual dream and myth of Canada. These young people bear the burden of immigrating their family and end up exploited.

Canadian universities, overflowing with immigrants and children of immigrants, say they need more foreign students. Because diversity. Anyone who believes that there is a shortage of cultural diversity in university has never been to one. Foreign youth are being used as cash cows. Unfortunately, many do not have that much cash to begin with.

Political Correctness

A white person could not have written this book. It is forbidden. This book is already politically incorrect, with its criticism of multiculturalism and Canada in general. Only my 'lived experience' as a brown immigrant permits me to write this uncouth content.

Officially, all Canadians are subject to the same laws. In practice, political correctness creates various castes with different social rules. Some rules benefit white people, some benefit coloured, some men, some women, and so on.

Speech is one of the areas of public life most impacted by political correctness. As an example, Toronto Mayor John Tory on May 28, 2020, proclaimed a Menstrual Health Day for "people who menstruate", calling them "menstruators" and never using the word women.[50] Using the word "women" could be offensive since there are other genders who menstruate. It is becoming normal for politicians to speak in a cautious, calculated, approved Canadian English. Average Canadians are also finding themselves pressured to speak and act within ever narrower accepted standards. Immigrants, like any other group, tend to focus on the social standards that hinder them or are new to them. This level of controlled speech is very new to newcomers.

It is becoming especially entrenched in the workplace. While intended to protect minorities and prevent harm, political correctness is creating fear. Not fear of causing offence, but fear of punishment. Saying or writing the wrong thing can be cause for termination. Even if it happens outside of the workplace and work time.

What exactly is the wrong thing to say or correct term to use is another headache for newcomers. Many are still learning English and can't keep up with fast changing terminology. 'Racialized person' is now the correct term that replaced 'minority', which replaced 'ethnic' which replaced 'coloured'. Next year, 'racialized' will be supplanted by another more correct term.

For many immigrants, there is a fear of speaking, of having the wrong views. Opinions are only spoken to family or to others within your ethnic group and in your language. Consequently, political correctness is fueling ethnic segregation. The risk of causing offence or being punished is higher than the benefit of new friends and cultural exchange. Cultural exchange might also be mistaken for cultural appropriation, so better to avoid it altogether.

Democracy is also being degraded. In a free country, the average person could discuss and engage in politics, hold office, and affect change. Now incorrect political opinions are dangerous to have or speak. Politics is best left to a ruling class with a polished command of approved Canadian English, holding the correct opinions.

Newcomers want to integrate in Canadian society and succeed in their career. Excessive political correctness adds another layer of dogma, difficulty, and fear to the already burdensome process of immigration.

Soviet Poster: Don't talk!

Slav Slaves

The English word *slave* ultimately comes from *Slav,* the eastern European peoples. Eastern Europeans were enslaved by Vikings, Magyars, Byzantines, Arabs, Turks, etc. for so many centuries that their name became the word for slave in many European languages. Even in recent history these people were invaded by Nazis and occupied by Soviets.

Eastern European immigrants in Canada came with this historical baggage. Many lived through Soviet socialist controlled societies, where there was only one approved political point of view. These countries were nominally democratic, with elections and parliaments. But speaking the wrong politics could cost your job, apartment or worse.

With Canada becoming more politically correct, many eastern Europeans have seen this movie before. While immigrants of colour are visible minorities and retain certain freedoms, Slavs are not. Eastern Europeans newcomers are white and get the worst of both worlds. Historical oppression, struggles of immigration, discrimination, all while thrown into the *white majority* category. As with other white people, they must watch what they say.

Careful speech is incredibly difficult for Slavs. Since the fall of communism their societies have become plain spoken, candid and rude. In addition to learning English, Slavic newcomers must learn the rules of approved white Canadian speech. Fake, polite, obedient speech.

Conforming to this politically correct society is infuriating to Slavic newcomers. Back home, many were forced to learn Russian in school and follow socialist 'comrade engineer' speech codes. The belief that Canada is a free country was a primary motivation for many to immigrate. Balancing their whiteness and immigrant status in a nervous and pretensive society leaves some wishing they were back in Bulgaria.

Indentured Immigration

Jamaican workers in Niagara Region (photo: AV Elkaim, New York Times)

Most everyone knows the story of Moses and the Exodus. Or at least have seen the movie *The Ten Commandments (1956).* The Hebrews were enslaved in Egypt until God told Moses to tell Pharaoh to let the people go. Few understand how the Hebrews ended up in Egyptian bondage in the first place. They immigrated to Egypt, voluntarily. Famine caused them to migrate into Egypt, where there was plenty of food and land.

For many immigrants, coming to the land of plenty and ending up in bondage is a familiar story. "We were treated like slaves" said Jamaican migrant worker Leon Ferguson, as reported by the Toronto Star in 2017.[51]

In America; racist, exploitative, bad America, Mexican agricultural workers are used for their cheap labour, sometimes abused and then sent back to where they came from. It doesn't happen in Canada of course, it's not possible.

The use and abuse of Temporary Foreign Workers in Canada is both widely reported and widely ignored. Most of the reporting is done by left leaning media and organizations. Since leftists now complain about everything under the sun, the few important issues they raise gets lost in the cacophony.

The Temporary Foreign Worker Program allows employers in Canada to hire temporary migrants. Canada is so venerated overseas, even temporary low wage work draws hundreds of thousands. Doing tedious work for low pay is not criminal in itself, but this program is surrounded by fraud and abuse. Some workers pay recruiters thousands of dollars for the chance at a low wage job in Canada. Paying for a job is illegal in Canada, but many recruiters are overseas. As reported by The Star (2017), a woman from the Philippines borrowed $6,000 to pay a recruiter to get her a job. She ended up packing vegetables for minimum wage in Ontario. Renewing work permits is another opportunity for recruiters to charge thousands. These workers can end up in debt bondage, working to pay the cost of getting a job.

Once in Canada and working, they are now dependent on the employer. Any complaints of conditions or reporting of abuse and their job could be terminated. They would also have to leave the country. After loss of employment, some choose to stay on undocumented.

Being illegal in Canada only introduces more opportunities for them to be abused or exploited.

The story of Leon Ferguson shows how disposable migrant workers can be, as recounted by The Star:

"He was hired to pick produce in a Kingsville greenhouse, but says his employer instead assigned him to do construction work. He says his bunkhouse with one bathroom and a two-burner stove was shared with eight other workers... Two months after Ferguson arrived in Canada, he says he injured his neck while lifting heavy stones outside the greenhouse.

He says his doctor recommended several months of treatment. But he says his employer tried to send him back to Jamaica almost immediately — and cancelled his health card."

Everyone knows migrant workers are used in this manner in the oil kingdoms of the middle east or the commercial farms of southern California. But not in Canada. We choose to not see our indentured immigrants. Migrant workers can see Canada but can't live Canada. As rich newcomers are wanted for their money, these foreign workers are wanted for their cheap, disposable labour. With all the kumbaya about immigration and multiculturalism, this indentured class of migrants get forgotten and they know it. They also know some Canadians resent them for keeping wages low and taking *their* jobs. Many regret their decision to come here, for them the land of bondage.

Television and Media

Canadian television can be summed up by one show: *Anne with an E.* The series is better titled *Anne with an Ideology*. It is government subsidized, redundant, politically correct art. Like most else in this category of art, *Anne with an E* is produced by the Canadian Broadcasting Corporation (CBC).

The series is another reboot of the classic Canadian book *Anne of Green Gables.* This time it's more in tune with current politics. Anne is predictably fighting the patriarchy and dealing with issues of anti-Black and anti-indigenous racism.

Canadian television is a small country's TV. Funded by the government and obedient to the prevailing ideology. In larger nations art is politically brave and can pay its own way. In smaller or medium sized countries, the government ensures that 'local' culture is seen on TV. Instead of art coming from the rebellious hearts of artists, it is funded and directed by a state bureau. Canadian bureaucrats insist that this is needed to avoid being swamped by American media. In 2019, CBC CEO Catherine Tait compared Netflix to colonialism.[52] Once again, the small colony of Canada struggling for its independence.

Canadian media must include a certain amount of Canadian content, to avoid us becoming even more Americanized. Even the CBC's own programming pokes fun at Canadian media's attempt to foster patriotism. *This hour has 22 minutes* included a sketch (2016) where they describe *Heritage Minutes* as "a commercial the government makes to make [Canada] seem like this is a real place."[53]

The CBC defines Canadian media. In a 2010 poll, 42% of Canadians considered the CBC an important national symbol.[54] They should. The government gives the CBC more than a billion dollars per year.[55]

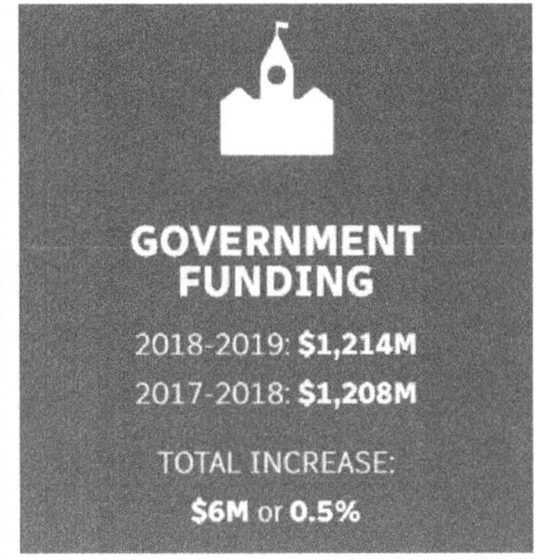

CBC's low revenue & high government funding

Not all national symbols are good or worth billions in funding. Many immigrants watch CBC programming as a guide for integration in Canadian society. What they see is underwhelming programming with a political slant. As William Watson writes in the Financial Post (2019), The CBC's *The National* produces "all the news that fits in the very narrow ideological spectrum of downtown-urban wokeness." Watson defines CBC's news four essential ingredients: climate, anti-Trump, Lefty-heroic, indigenous.[56]

Many newcomers do not know that they are paying for the CBC and funding Canadian media. In 2019, the Liberal government planned to give another $600 million in subsidies to media outlets. The proposal was to support journalism. But many suspect the plot is to bribe the media in return for partisan coverage. Just like the old country.[57]

Anyone who uses cable or satellite TV in this country pays a subsidy to create Canadian content. The Canada Media Fund, another patriotic surtax. Layers of taxpayer funding, involuntary consumer funding and regulations on content. Media in Canada is expensive mediocrity.

Cost of Living

Newcomers expect that Canada will be more expensive to live in. Rich countries normally have a higher cost of living, with higher incomes to match. This is largely due to the higher cost of labour, a key economic input. Immigrants are still shocked at how much more expensive life is in Canada. Unnecessary expenses are added to the cost of living. Subsidizing the media is just one example of a bourgeois cost imposed on taxpayers.

The usual explanation for extra costs is Canada's large geography and low population density. However Australia, a rich country with an even lower population density has lower cell phone rates than Canada.[58]

There is a long list of higher priced items in Canada compared to its peers. Much of it is due to the oligopolies that dominate the Canadian economy. Prime examples include banking and telecoms. Government is usually the direct cause of the rest. High income taxes, consumption taxes, rising property taxes, gas taxes, regulations on everything.

No one should mourn the high cost of sins such as alcohol or tobacco. But housing, heating, and car insurance are unnecessarily costlier.

A good example is the cost of hydro, what we call electricity in Ontario. As CBC News (2017) recounted:

"The report by the Fraser Institute, which used data from Statistics Canada, shows from 2008 to 2016 residential hydro costs in Ontario rose 71 per cent, while the average increase across Canada totalled 34 per cent."

"Policy choices by the Ontario government have been the leading drivers of increased prices," reads the report. It blames the continued generation of an excess supply of power despite diminishing demand, as well as the Liberal government's decisions to pay premium prices to spur wind and solar energy development in the province.[59]

These burdens fall heavily on the poor and those on pensions. Life in Canada is made more expensive by policy choices. Since we elect our governments, policy choices made by Canadians.

ment   FP Picks   Investing   Markets   Economy   Entrepreneur   Real Estate   Commodities

Retail & Marketing / News

Canada's grocery oligopoly missed a glorious opportunity and may now pay the price one way or another

Kevin Carmichael: The big grocers could still be facing trouble even if the Competition Bureau lets them off the hook

Kevin Carmichael

Jul 15, 2020 • Last Updated 3 months ago • 4 minute read

Obedient Complacency

Most Canadians know they're overpaying for goods and government. They simply accept it as part of life in Canada. They do not want costly policy decisions but will also never vote against them. Canadians don't oppose. Canadians do and say what they're supposed to.

Many newcomers find Canadian culture to be on the obedient side of the spectrum. Less than Germany and Japan. But much more than the United States, Latin America, India, the Middle East and Africa.

There is a complacency and deference in Canada that borders on serfdom. One theory says this is part of Canada's history. When the American colonies revolted and broke away from British rule, some were still loyal to the Crown. Many loyalists moved north into British Canada. They formed the core of Canada's loyal and obedient culture. While independent America declared the rights of *life, liberty and the pursuit of happiness,*

Canada would function in the name of *peace, order, and good government*.

Looking back, author and academic Michael Ignatieff once said, "we have sacrificed too much freedom for the sake of order."[60] Journalist Andrew Cohen (2017) stated "Canadians are captains of complacency," asking "Why are we so timid?" This culture stifles economic innovation and political debate.[61]

For immigrants, Canadian culture can seem too ordered and orthodox. Many of us come from chaotic parts of the world and struggle to adapt to a 'supposed to' society. Canadian conformity is also confusing since it is the opposite of official multiculturalism. Keeping your messy foreign culture is not a good idea in clean Canada.

Smug Life

Canadian complacency can be expanded into another word, smug. The best and most pluralist country in the world. The antithesis to Donald Trump. One reason immigrants flock to Canada is because its reputation overseas is even better than it is in Canada. A difficult feat to pull off since Canada thinks so highly of itself.

When Black protestors demonstrate against institutional racism in America, Canadians understand and support them. But if someone alleges systemic discrimination in Canada, we scratch our heads in confusion. When American and European banks collapse in crisis, when their housing markets crash, we don't lose any sleep. Our institutions are strong and well regulated. Canada always thinks itself well governed, tolerant, diverse, and open. No one has a prouder Pride Parade or a more colourful Caribana.

Writer Luke Savage calls this *maple washing*. "The realities of Canada prove less important in our national discourse than the comforting illusions we celebrate." Our sanitized national narrative.[62]

Columnist J.J. McCullough explained, "To grow up in Canada is to be endlessly bombarded with folk tales of Canadians' legendary politeness, kindness and obedience." Explaining how our ego was put to use to fight the Covid-19 pandemic, McCullough cited the Toronto Star: "our national DNA favours the collective during a crisis that has demanded collective action, mutual sacrifice, looking out for the other rather than insistence on personal liberty and pursuit of happiness." McCullough's article was a rare breath of fresh air, questioning our character. "Living day-to-day life in Canada also means experiencing a place dramatically at odds with such sentimentalism, a country of people lying to the return counter, swearing at each other in the parking lot and puking outside the club." McCullough writes: "If you know you're going to be praised for being a paragon of politeness and empathy regardless of what you do, you may as well just behave the way you want."[63]

Slowly but surely the international media that sings Canada's praise is also gaining some colour. *Vice Media* published an article "Dear Canada, Stop Being So Goddam Smug." And *The Guardian*: "Think Canada is a progressive paradise? That's moose shit."

Newcomers often get sold on the ideal country myth. Many left their families and homes for a chance to live in the perfect country. Only to find out it's a self-righteous country. Their inevitable disappointment will propel them to speak out. Or at least warn other potential immigrants. But no one will believe them. Canadians or foreigners alike. They must fit in and avoid seeming ungrateful.

According to J.J. McCullough, smug is our national emotion.

Choice Supportive Bias

Newcomers to Canada leave behind a lot for the privilege of immigrating. It's a long and expensive process. After coming to Canada, many end up having to justify their decision. To family members and to themselves.

Choice supportive bias is the tendency to retroactively assign positive attributes to an option selected or decision made.[64] In this case, the decision to move to Canada. Immigrants must believe that Canada is a wonderful country. Or at least they have to say it to others. To criticize Canada would be to criticize the decision they made and admit a big mistake.

Sometimes a husband or wife was the main persuader in bringing the family to Canada. If the other spouse didn't want to immigrate, you better believe you're now in the best country in the world. Or your wife was right.

Other relatives back home also need to be reassured that you didn't screw up. You must put up a front that your new life is worth it. That you're successful in candy-coated Canada. And because you confirmed to everyone how great Canada is, now they want to immigrate also. The cycle of candy-coated-immigration.

This post-purchase rationalization can cause problems within families or within individual's heads. For many immigrants, there is a dissonance between the reality of life in Canada and what we want to believe about Canada. For those who have the option of returning to their home country, this choice supportive bias stops them from going back. Some however, don't have that option, even if they can get over the shame of un-emigrating. They sold what they had and spent too much coming here, with nothing to return to.

Our national policy making also suffers. Evidence-based decision-making gives way to confirmation bias, choice-supportive bias and the lies immigrants join in telling.

Assimilation

We'll be wiped out before long. My brother is married to an American girl and he has a son. There is no more hope. We are trying to forget Assyria.

William Saroyan wrote this in 1934, describing an Assyrian immigrant in America. He feared being wiped out, by violence in Iraq and assimilation into Western culture.[65]

Topics of immigration tend to be dominated by larger groups, the Chinese, Indians, Nigerians. Smaller ethnicities have their own problems. Armenians and Assyrians for example have smaller populations and are conscious of it. They are conscious of it because those low numbers are the surviving population of massacres.

These communities find a haven in the Western world. Here they live in peace and prosperity, but also worry about assimilation. With each new generation, fewer children learn the old language. Some marry outside of the community. Eventually they simply melt into white society.

Cultural suicide is a controversial term, but it is a concern for some immigrants.[66] Keeping their identity is not a preference, it's a survival instinct, sharpened through tragedy and genocide. By coming to Canada, they know their children would survive. But their children might one day assimilate too much into North American culture and forget the old identity. Whether or not this counts as survival is debated within the community. Some cultures remain tight knit and sometimes look down upon assimilation. As Montreal Armenian psychiatrist Taline Zourikian put it, "we don't assimilate."[67]

Even for immigrants who aren't concerned with the survival of their community, assimilation poses a problem. Becoming 'white-washed' is sometimes seen as an unfortunate consequence of immigrating to countries like Canada. Mainstream white culture is seen as spoilt, materialistic, hollow, and in some areas effeminate.

Proud and sometimes macho immigrants don't want their children to assimilate into a decadent Western society.

In 1925 a US court ruled Tatos Catozian could receive citizenship. The court found Armenians were white, partly because they "readily amalgamate with the European and white races."

Small town Canada

Most immigrants move to the major metropolitan centres like the Greater Toronto and Vancouver areas. A few however end up in small towns that even most born-in-Canada Canadians never heard of. Like everything else in immigration, the relationship with small towns is complex. Newcomers have reasons to both love and hate small town Canada.

Several towns actively try to attract international newcomers. Many small town youth leave to go to university in big cities and don't come back. Some just plain leave. A few small communities are at risk of disappearing over the next few decades. When the only elementary school shuts down, the writing is on the wall.

Immigrants are sometimes expected to save these towns. They bring money, labour, entrepreneurialism. Welcome to our community, please get to work saving us from decline. This task falls on newcomers who are busy uprooting from their old country and integrating in a new land. And if this rescue experiment fails, immigrants will probably get the blame. There is a quid pro quo, you can come here if you help revitalize the community. If local decline persists, then why did we let you come here? To take the few jobs left? Unfortunately, some towns will decline whether or not immigrants contribute their full potential. The optimism of revitalization will be lost and only xenophobia could be left.[68]

Hopefully newcomers can and will help renew these small communities. There is a lot of potential in this match making. Many immigrants come from traditional cultures where the extended family and local community are vital. They should fit in to the small townships where everyone knows everyone. Housing is usually much more affordable and the simpler pace of life leaves more time for integrating into the local scene.

What newcomers will lose is the cultural kin that is found in the big cities. Your relatives probably live in the major metro centres, and they usually help much more with integrating newcomers. Another feature common in big cities that will be missed is the ethnic food stores. There aren't many Arab or Korean grocery stores in the hinterland.

Geography

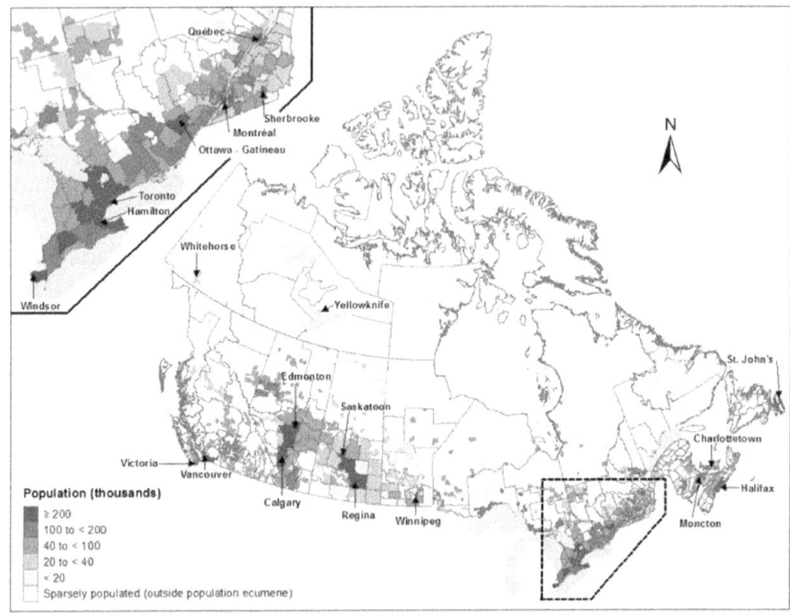

Source: Statistics Canada, Demography Division

A Mari usque ad Mare is the official motto of Canada, Latin for *From Sea to Sea*. Inspired from the Biblical Psalms, "He shall have dominion also from sea to sea, and from the river unto the ends of the earth".

When Canada was confederated in 1867 it was the ambition that the nation would stretch from the Atlantic to the Pacific Ocean. Soon that vast expanse would be

Canadian and the motto would not be enough to describe the sheer size of this country. From sea to sea to sea, now seems appropriate, adding the Arctic Ocean. The second half of the Psalmist verse already represents Northern Canada, with much of the Arctic seeming like the ends of the earth.

The vast majority of Canadians live in the southern strip of Canada that sticks close to the American border. Immigrants especially cluster in Southern Canada, if there is such a thing. Newcomers are usually too busy getting their career started to do much travelling. But when they do start to explore Canada, the enormous size of this land is overwhelming. The second largest country by geography, distance between cities is measured by hours of driving or flying. In some cases, it's easier to see famous American landmarks or visit family in the home country than to travel within Canada.

The desire to be Canadian is tempered by the cost, in time and money, of knowing this immense land. Most newcomers will never travel more than a few places in this country. Settling on common and close to home trips like driving from Toronto to Niagara Falls. Living in a country without truly experiencing it can be depressing. Immigrants hate having to explain to family in the old country that they have never been to Montreal or Winnipeg. Never seen the Rocky Mountains or the red soil of Prince Edward Island. And it reminds them that maybe they can never be fully Canadian.

With a country spread out across a continent, the provinces develop their own unique cultures. Scott Gilmore writes that Canada is a nation of strangers. "Every region, every province, sits in isolation". Only 15% of Canadians live outside their province of birth. Contrast that with 30%-40% of Americans who live in a state other than their birth state.[69] Vacationing is also more likely an overseas adventure than inter-Canadian.

Adding to the challenge is the fact that Canada is frozen and dark one third of the year. Some Canadians suffer from Seasonal Affective Disorder (SAD), a kind of depression. Commonly called 'winter blues', it's believed to be caused by the lack of sunlight.

It is difficult for immigrants to become Canadian when *Canada* simply means Greater Toronto or Vancouver. Geography is a barrier for newcomers who will always feel like an alien in this land they do not know.

Century Initiative

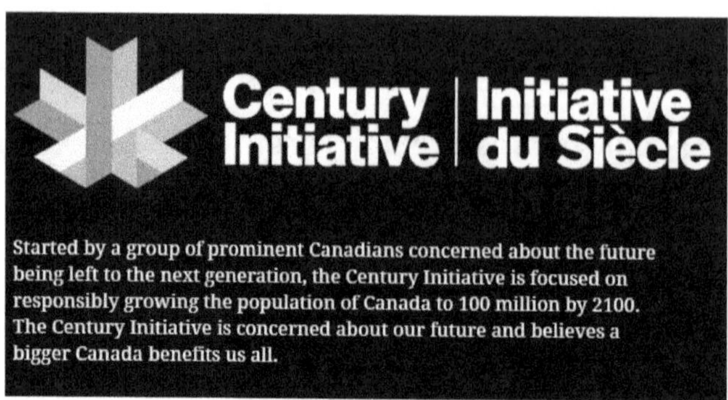

If you never heard of the Century Initiative, it's basically the opposite of Malthusianism. In 1798, Reverend Thomas Malthus wrote that human population growth is exponential and would outstrip food production and other resources. Modern environmentalists take a similar view that there are too many people on a planet struggling to support them.

The Century Initiative is the opposite and Canada specific version of this. It says that Canada has too few people and a big geography that can support much more. The grand idea is to increase immigration and fertility to get

Canada's population to 100 million by the year 2100. "For a bigger, bolder Canada" is their slogan.[70]

Population is always a comparative concern. People in smaller countries think there are too much of *them*: China, India, Brazil, USA. And not enough of *us*: Canada, Uruguay, Singapore. The world be a better place if there were more of us, and less of them. Canadians especially have this moral superiority complex. 'The world needs more Canada' the title of a famous book and slogan for new-age imperialism. This highlights one of the main reasons for large scale immigration, the great Canadian ego.

Another important reason Canada has had high rates of immigration is the corporate lobby. It is no coincidence that the founders of the Century Initiative are all business leaders. Hailing from McKinsey & Co, Cisco Canada, the Business Council of Canada, Blackrock Alternative Investors. Immigration in Canada is a capitalist enterprise. More consumers to demand, more labour to supply, more profit.

It doesn't take newcomers long to realise they are needed (if not used) to keep real estate, the stock market and the labour force growing. Someone must pay pensions for aging white people. Someone must do the odd jobs and keep wages under control.

Newcomers arrive here thinking that they have won the privilege of coming to Canada. Then realize that the pharaohs of commerce brought them to build pyramids.

An important question for the Century Initiative is what's the real agenda. Is the goal to create a big country using higher levels of immigration? Or is mass migration the actual goal, using the big country ego as a pretext.

Even if we create a larger country using more newcomers, would we be a cohesive nation? Canada is already a 'nation of strangers' as Gilmore puts it. Packing more newcomers into the big cities is likely to reinforce ethnic enclaves, impede integration, and strain municipal services.

Canada is back

Prime Minister Justin Trudeau (centre, pink shirt, at Montreal Pride Parade)

When Justin Trudeau and his Liberal Party won the 2015 federal election, he made a declaration to Canada's friends all around the world.

*"Many of you have worried that Canada has lost its compassionate & constructive voice in the world over the past 10 years. Well, I have a simple message for you: **on behalf of 35 million Canadians, we're back.**"*[71]

The previous 10 years was under the Conservative Party's Stephen Harper. How someone so apparently un-Canadian like Harper managed to win the 2008 and 2011 elections is unimaginable. Canadians must have sleepwalked into voting booths those two times.

Canada, you see, is *supposed to* vote Liberal. The Conservative Party is un-Canadian.

A clarification for Europeans and Australians, the Liberal party is left-of-centre, and the Conservative Party is right-of-centre.

The Liberal Party considers itself the natural governing party of Canada. Actually, the Liberal Party considers itself Canada. They governed almost 70 years of the 20th century.[72] When Trudeau stated that Canada was back after his Party was returned to power, he meant what he said. The Liberal Party has a successful strategy binding the Party's brand to what it means to be Canadian.

For some immigrants this is another example of Canadian pretenses. Democratic pretenses in this case.

Most dictatorships and autocracies have elections and political parties. Communist China, the former East Germany and Syria all have these veneers of democracy. But in these countries only one party is supposed to win and govern.

'The Party and the State is One' is a dangerous and egotistical idea. It leads to corruption and abuse of power when one group thinks they have a divine right to rule. Many newcomers come from crooked countries with fraudulent elections and ruling elites. Seeing a political party in Canada with a heavenly mandate is disappointing.

In 2013, Justin Trudeau was asked which country's administration he most admired. His response was in line with one-party-rule and central planning.

"There's a level of admiration I actually have for China because their basic dictatorship is allowing them to actually turn their economy around on a dime & say, 'We need to go green … we need to start investing in solar."[73]

There are two major demographics that the Liberal Party relies on. Firstly, the female vote. According to Abacus Data, the female vote was won by 17 points in 2015.[74]

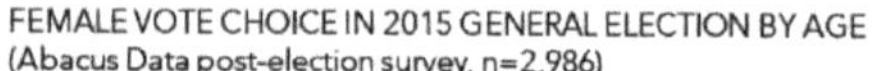

LIBERALS WON ALL FEMALE AGE GROUPS. MARGIN GREATER AMONG YOUNGER WOMEN.

FEMALE VOTE CHOICE IN 2015 GENERAL ELECTION BY AGE
(Abacus Data post-election survey, n=2,986)

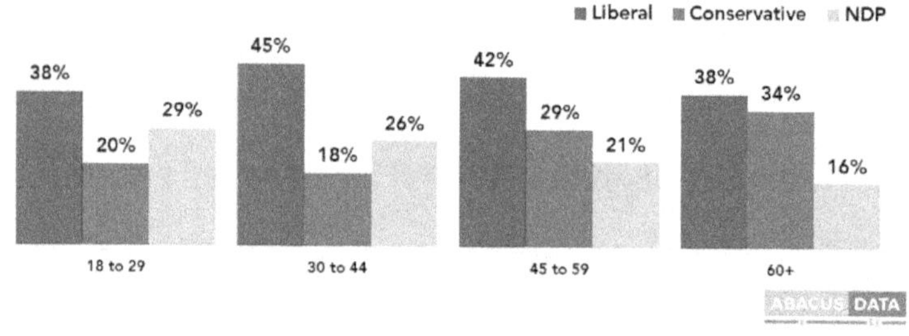

The other demographic is of course, immigrants. We have been told by many immigrant uncles: we are supposed to vote Liberal, "or we wouldn't be here." Even the name *Trudeau* is sacred for older generations of immigrants. Pierre Trudeau, Justin's father, gets the credit for opening immigration in Canada and enshrining multiculturalism.

Some younger immigrants and those who vote NDP, Conservative or Green, hate the idea that we are supposed to vote a certain way. Especially when implied that we owe eternal gratitude to the celestial Party for bringing us to the Northern Kingdom.

The irony of immigrants devotedly voting Liberal is that few of them are actually liberal or progressive. Some of the most racist, homophobic, misogynist, un-environmental immigrants are faithful followers of the Party. Credit must be given to the Liberals for holding together a political coalition of white feminists and Arabian clerics.

The Liberal's success in ruling for decades and binding their brand to the nation has a downside for the Party. The Liberals have become the establishment in Canada. Criticism of the Canadian establishment is mostly criticism of Liberal ideology. Canadian failings, such as systemic discrimination, un-integrated immigrants, neglected First Nations, deficits and debt can be placed at the State Party's feet.

Deficits and Debt

Intergenerational fairness is an idea gaining traction in the discussion of national finances. At least before the coronavirus pandemic threw residual notions of fiscal responsibility out the window. It's the idea that government deficits and debt need to be considered not only from a financial point of view, but through a demographic lens as well. As Parisa Mahboubi from the C.D. Howe Institute writes:

"Generational accounting is a powerful tool for assessing the lifetime fiscal burden on current and future generations, given demographic and economic projections... A large imbalance between the net tax burden faced by current and future generations over their lifetimes, in favor of current generations, would mean that existing fiscal policies are unfair and unsustainable."[75]

In other words, governments spending large amounts of borrowed money today benefits current Canadians, at the expense of future generations. Future generations bear the cost of high deficits and debt. Interest payments can take up large sections of the budget which would otherwise go to health or education. Higher taxes may be needed to pay the cost of the higher debt load.

Almost all analysis of intergenerational government finances is focused on younger Canadians versus the baby boomers or whoever borrowed and spent the most money. It is often forgotten that new immigrants are also responsible for paying the costs of government debt. As we get off the plane, we inherit these costs, money spent and enjoyed years before we got here. New Canadians will be paying the financial debt of old Canadians.

When immigration enters the discussion of deficits and debt, it's unashamedly a solution to the problem of who will pay. The C.D. Howe Institute's analysis is littered with immigrants helping to pay the state's accumulated debt:

- "immigration can be an effective way to mitigate the burden…"
- "fiscal sustainability requires that the immigration rate remains high…"

The C.D. Howe Institute is better than most, adding caveats that newcomers have difficulty entering the labour market, and that immigration alone can't solve fiscal problems. Less rigorous articles almost always use newcomers as an easy fix to the problem of a state living beyond its means. Implying that since the problem can be easily solved, it isn't really a problem.

In 2020, Canada is living up to this philosophy that excessive state borrowing is nothing to worry about. According to an International Monetary Fund (IMF) projection, Canada is on track to have the highest deficit of any country.[76] Canadian exceptionalism, this time in economic fantasy. As is our custom, this gathering storm is widely reported but also widely ignored.

Why worry about fiscal responsibility when we have newcomers to help finance the accumulated debt.

Future Canadians, babies and immigrants, will be paying for our past spending. Whether or not they benefit from that spending will depend on how farsighted our governments are. Bring as much money as you can.

Foreign Aid

Most immigrants come from developing countries, such as China, India, the Philippines and Nigeria. In 2019, Canada spent approximately $6.4 billion on what is formally called *international assistance*.[77]

Foreign aid spending should be uncontroversial, especially to immigrants. That helpful cash is going to our home countries. Canada is a rich country and rich countries should help poor countries. Sounds good. Except when you tell an immigrant that Canada sends $6,000,000,000 overseas. The reaction is usually shock and confusion. That's *our* money, they say. It should be spent on hospital beds and schools in Canada. Medical care for veterans and clean water for First Nations.

Immigrants think foreign aid spending is too much. The same immigrants will send money via Western Union to family in the old country every year. Occasionally many times during the year; birthdays, Christmas or whenever there is a sad story.

Immigrants basically want foreign aid privatized to them. This is not as odd as it sounds. We know the recipients personally, who is deserving and who is not. We know the charities that can be trusted and the services we used in the old country. We also know how ineffective governments can be, especially in the developing world. Another reason immigrants hate foreign aid is they think this is another vanity project for Canada. Canada is always trying to project a benevolent image at taxpayers' expense.

Immigrants are taxpayers in Canada and react the way a taxpayer should. Sticker shock at the price tag, then thinking there must be a better way of doing this.

Hate for other countries is another reason for hatred of foreign aid. Why is Canada giving money to *that* country? They're Muslim, they're communist, those people are a waste of money, or they're rich and fooling everyone.

Foreign Policy

The Gardiner Expressway is a major and iconic highway in Toronto. Traffic was business as usual until May 10th, 2009 when a few thousand Tamil protestors rushed the onramps to blockade the highway. Mothers with children in strollers included. With the worsening civil war in Sri Lanka, the Tamils were calling for the Canadian government to intervene.[78]

With so many immigrants and children of immigrants in Canada, the affairs of the rest of the world are now here. International issues would repeatedly become local protests to the Canadian government. Lebanese opposed to Israeli bombing, Persians opposed to the Iran regime, dissidents against Russia, China, Venezuela and America.

Immigrants expect to pressure the Canadian government to take their side in whatever conflict is happening overseas. Even when the government does act, it is usually just symbolic. A carefully balanced statement is issued. Unimpressed and unsatisfied, immigrants blame Canada for being weak or uncaring of their plight back home.

Armenian diaspora in Canada says Ottawa must act to prevent a second genocide

Published Oct. 12, 2020 2:56 p.m. ET

Share this story:  f

MONTREAL - The ongoing conflict between Armenia and Azerbaijan is physically and emotionally distant to most Canadians, but for Montrealer Talar Chichmanian, the war is the second time since the 1990s her family has taken up arms.

In 2020, as the Armenian-Azerbaijan conflict rekindled, the diaspora once again blamed Canada for not doing enough. As CP24 reported, Montreal Armenian Talar Chichmanian called on the Canadian government to support the Armenian side. "Normally, I'm proud to call myself Canadian, but this past week has been a horrible disappointment."[79]

Sometimes the government not only fails to support a side, but also designates the overseas 'freedom fighters' as terrorist organizations. This prevents immigrants from helping that particular struggle. These immigrants see Canada as siding with harsh regimes and helping to oppress their people.

Canada cannot please all factions and cannot intervene overseas. Due to the scale of immigration and its diversity, there are many factions. Each conflict overseas, each uprising against a regime results in a group of indignant immigrants in Canada.

Refugees

Immigration is multi-tiered in Canada. Rich investors, skilled workers, family class, and refugees. There's something unpleasant about the word *refugee.* Even other immigrants look down their nose at them.

The immigration process is long, arduous and expensive. Refugees are seen as getting easy entry into Canada. Lucky them. Then there is skepticism. Are they *real* refugees? Or just smart enough to skip the lines.

Surveys of Canadians consistently show skepticism of refugees. In 2010, 59% of Canadians agreed with the statement *"Many people claiming to be refugees are not real refugees."*[80] In 2018 as 'irregular migrants' were crossing from the US border, only 27% of those polled believed most of the people crossing were genuine refugees.[81]

Another way to understand the way refugees are viewed is to look at the *perceived* number of refugees or humanitarian class of immigrants. Canadians think 30%

of immigrants are refugees, while the actual number is

15%.[82]

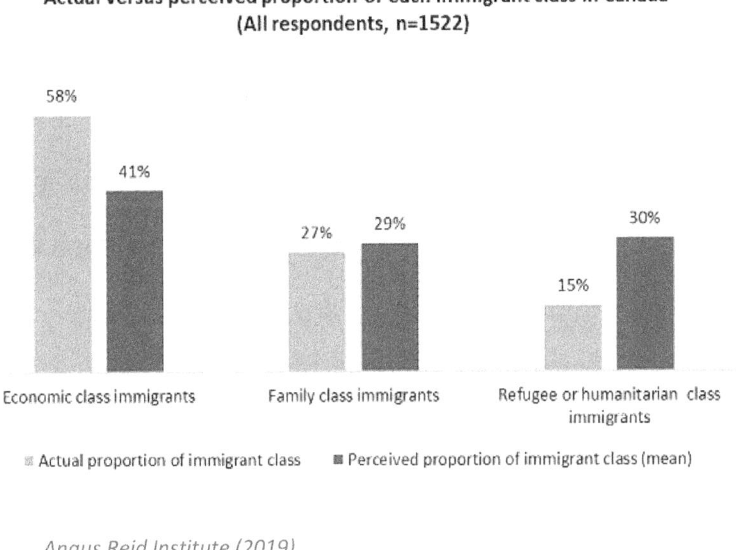

Angus Reid Institute (2019)

In addition to thinking refugees are getting an easy ticket

into Canada, immigrants are skeptical of refugees for

two more reasons. First, the Canadian preference for

highly skilled and richer newcomers has created a class

schism between rich and poor migrants. Most

newcomers are now middle class (at least in their home

countries) and have little taste for identifying with huddled masses of refugees.

Another reason is the immigration process itself. Newcomers are familiar with the complex and meandering process. There are embellishments, padding and untruths that go into an immigration application. If we lied about our bank account to come to Canada, they must be doing it too. Immigrants don't trust our immigration system to properly evaluate refugees. Furthermore, the perception that refugees get a shortcut is a bitter reminder of the grueling and costly immigration process.

Consultants

The bright shine that radiates from Canada is enough to lure immigrants and refugees halfway across the world. That shine is partly invented by people selling immigration. The marketing of Canada is complex. It is sold as a Christian country to Christian minorities. A LGBT haven to oppressed gays. A real estate market for the rich. And a jobs depot for poor people. From students to plumbers, every niche is covered.

While some consultants do provide honest help in navigating the complex process of immigration, separating the good from the bad is difficult.

Fraud and abuse of immigrants and applicants is common. Even after arriving in Canada, there is post-traumatic stress from dealing with sometimes corrupt agents and consultants.

The immigration consultancy business is so lucrative that squabbles often break out over who gets to regulate the industry. A list of regulatory bodies has claimed authority over the years.

The Canadian Society of Immigration Practitioners (CSIP), Canadian Society of Immigration Consultants (CSIC), Immigration Consultants of Canada Regulatory Council (ICCRC), College of Immigration and Citizenship Consultants (CICC).

The federal government had recognized the CSIC, until "issues with CSIC's governance and accountability." The ICCRC was then selected to replace the failing CSIC, and now the CICC is supposed to replace the ICCRC.[83]

Shady agents aren't the only ones fraudulently selling the Canadian Dream. Some Canadians can't resist contributing to the fake marketing. Prime Minister Justin

Trudeau added his display of Canadian faux openness. In January 2017, he tweeted *"to those fleeing persecution, terror & war, Canadians will welcome you, regardless of your faith. Diversity is our strength #WelcometoCanada."*[84]

Between the 2017 tweet and the Covid-19 crisis, over 50,000 irregular migrants crossed from the US. They were soon to find out, it's not as simple as Trudeau's welcome hashtag. Of the 28,644 refugee claims finalized, only half were accepted. 42% were rejected, 3% were abandoned, and 5% were withdrawn/other. Another 29,605 claims were still pending. Thousands of migrants were trekking to Canada on false hopes. Spending what little money they had or borrowed. False hopes advertised by people selling Canada.[85]

Statistics on refugee claims made by Irregular Border Crossers, by Calendar Year and Quarter

National	Intake	Accepted	Rejected	Abandoned	Withdrawn & Other	Total Finalized	Pending
				Finalized			
Total	58,255	14,420	11,948	938	1,338	28,644	29,605

Immigration & Refugee Board of Canada, mid 2020

Legal System

In 2009, David Chen ran a small grocery shop in Toronto's Chinatown. Shoplifters were routinely stealing from Chinatown's shops. David Chen describes the "frustration of dying the death by a thousand cuts by shoplifters everyday." The Chinese community felt the police were not adequately responding to their concerns.

David Chen and two workers decided to act. They caught, tied up a shoplifter and called the police. When the police arrived, they arrested David Chen. He was charged with assault and forcible confinement for catching the thief.[86]

Many months later Chen was found not guilty. But the damage was done. For this community, insult was added to injury.

Newcomers are often impressed by the professional look of police, fire, and paramedics. Only to be later disappointed if these services don't live up to high expectations. Many immigrants feel that 'equal protection under the law' is only a theory. In practice they believe the police and judicial system treat them like second-class citizens. Some communities not only feel inadequate police protection, but also systemic discrimination with excessive police targeting.

Even for newcomers who are less critical of the legal system, there is uncertainty. Some are unsure whether they have a right to self-defence. And many believe criminals are afforded more rights than law abiding folk.

Occasionally, a new legal term appears that adds to the confusion. Such as when the murderer of an eight-year-old girl was moved from prison to a 'healing lodge'. In fact, between 2011 and 2018, more than 20 child murderers were transferred to 'healing lodges'. But this was a high-profile case, and many born Canadians were outraged.[87] Immigrants were not surprised. They've come to expect lenient and whimsical rulings from the judicial system.

The federal Department of Justice website cites a poll where 79% of Canadians think sentences are too lenient. With 65% believing the laws themselves are too soft. This has been a consistent view of Canadians for many years.[88] Layered on this is the lower confidence visible minorities hold in the system. According to a 2018 Angus Reid poll, minorities hold substantially less confidence in police and the courts.[89]

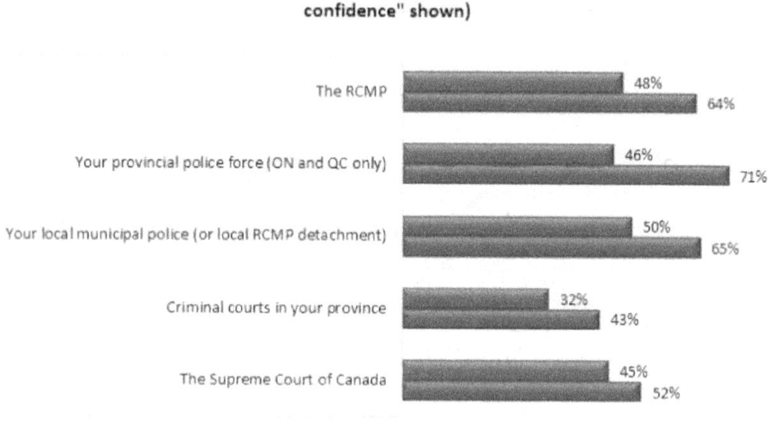

2018 Angus Reid Institute

Making the legal system more considerate of minorities is not as simple as it sounds. Diversity is our complication. A prime example of this came from the Law Society of Ontario (LSO), the body that governs Ontario's lawyers and paralegals. In 2016, the LSO passed a Statement of Principles resolution, requiring members to promote Diversity, Equality, and Inclusion. While the intent of this may have been to promote the interests of underprivileged groups, such as minorities and immigrants, it represented a conflict in the conscience of Canada. Some of the most progressive and experienced lawyers such as Murray Klippenstein and young aspiring immigrants, such as Teng Rong were opposed to this Statement of Principles requirement.

Klippenstein wrote: "the Law Society is demanding that I openly state that I <u>am adopting</u>, and <u>will promote</u>, and <u>will implement "generally" in my daily life</u>, two specific and pretty significant words or "principles", words that are quite vague but sound important." Adding he once believed freedom of thought, opinion and expression was an issue for people in far away countries.[90]

Immigrants like Teng Rong, can agree that far away countries control and compel their citizens. "For 10 years I slowly wiggled out of the grip of [Chinese] communist propaganda."

Rong writes "Canada is the last place I would have expected to see support for compelled speech."

"The LSO wants to make the expression of these principles a condition of continued employment in the legal profession. This is compelled speech, and I cannot in good conscience support it."[91]

After a few years of debate, in 2019 the LSO finally repealed this Statement of Principles. The Supreme Court of Canada long ago stated that forcing someone to express opinions that they do not have "is totalitarian and as such alien to the tradition of free nations like Canada."

The LSO's Statement of Principles episode demonstrated the challenge of incorporating diversity (and immigrants) while preserving individual rights. It is a paradox of immigration to Canada. Immigrants come here to be free, and in the name of accommodating them, there are attempts to reduce their freedom.

Politeness

When award winning Canadian author Yann Martel described Canada as the greatest hotel on earth, he meant it as a compliment[92]. Canada is so nice, so caring, so eager to please. The polite Hoteliers treat you like guests. In your home, your family treats you like a nobody. You would probably still choose to live long term in your home, with chores and rude family. Likewise, no one would risk their life to defend a hotel.

Hotel Canada is polite, but like all hotels it is an artificial home. A real home would be better. It may be less polite, but more real. Immigrants did not come to

Canada for a stay in a fancy hotel state. We could have gone to Dubai for that.

Excessive politeness is seen as fake by many newcomers. Eventually immigrants will come to realize the politeness can be passive aggressive behaviour. Used to insult and insinuate as much as to be gracious. It also serves to avoid difficult subjects, reality, or truth.

Like other annoyances, it blocks integration. Unnecessary use of "I'm sorry" is confusing to English language learners. Indirect language often goes misunderstood. In many cases, newcomers continue bad habits because they've never been directly told they're doing something wrong.

Another irritation is the fact that politeness is usually humble bragging. Canadians boast about how polite they are. Especially in comparison to those rude Americans. But immigrants are also from rude countries. Sneering at rude Americans is the same as sneering at rude Indians, Poles and Arabs. Canadians think they can despise rude America while politely respecting the rest of the world.

Making *I'm Sorry* our national identity is laughable to the rest of the world, and to newcomers. Canadian politeness is cosmetic and phony. It conceals our identity problem while highlighting the inferiority complex.

The unicorn and the unicorn

Canadian Coat of Arms

The unicorn on this book's cover is taken from the Canadian coat of arms. Which is derived from the British coat of arms. The lion and the unicorn representing England and Scotland. While most nations employ an eagle or beaver as their national animal, the Scots have a mythological beast.

Beast is the correct term for the unicorn. Symbolizing Scotland, the historical concept of a unicorn is proud, fierce, wild and untamed. This is the opposite of the modern understanding of unicorns. Now commonly used as a child's decorative toy, unicorns today are very much domestic. They are sparkly, friendly and pretty.

The contrasting images of this mythical creature mirror the identity of immigrants. To some, immigrants are barbarians, foreign and dangerous. To others, they represent tolerance, culture and a shared humanity.

Immigrants are of course both. They are of foreign origin, some with wild and hateful characteristics. But Canadian immigrants are mostly middle class and reasonably decent. Also, the idea of different peoples living together symbolizes peace on earth and goodwill toward men. Reconciling these conflicting views of newcomers is the challenge for ensuring immigration success in Canada.

There must be a common denominator that both sides can agree on. Whether immigrants are savages or symbols of harmony, our shared values are the key. Even barbarians value freedom and their pursuit of happiness.

Coat of Arms unicorns: Canadian (left) vs British (right)

The heraldic unicorn also symbolizes Canada as a nation. If one compares the unicorns on the Canadian coat of arms and the original British, the difference is notable.

The Canadian version is more muscular and burlier. It has teeth and hair on its face. Angry is the word that comes to mind looking at its demeanour. Its red tongue spitting fury. The Canadian unicorn is much closer to the fierce and untamed version of the mythical animal. Perhaps as a country we were meant to be angrier, with more animosity and opposition. Maybe even hate.

Alexander Lowen wrote that narcissists have a true and false self. The false self is the superficial façade presented to the world. While the true self is hidden and denied.[93] Perhaps the angry unicorn is Canada's true self, hidden behind the apologies, complacency, and political correctness.

Is Canada a narcissistic country? Overly concerned with its image as an open, tolerant space? Did we chain and imprison our fierce unicorn, replacing it with a pretty façade? For centuries, the conflict between the wild unicorn and attempts to tame and domesticate it has been depicted on British and now Canadian heraldry. The unicorn is shown with a chain flowing from its neck.

At the end of the chain it is open, disconnected and broken. The broken chain symbolizes its freedom and opposition to oppression. The chain itself demonstrates an attempt to control, domesticate and oppress the beast.

Identity

In 1949 on three Canadian Navy ships, scores of sailors refused to follow orders. A commission to investigate found among other reasons, the absence of a distinguishing Canadian identity in the Navy.[94] There are consequences of having or lacking a national identity. Decades later in 2015, Prime Minister Justin Trudeau proudly told a New York Times journalist "there is no core identity, no mainstream in Canada."[95]

Canada has long struggled with its identity. Made up of Indigenous, French, British, immigrants from everywhere else, stretched across a wide land, this is bound to happen.

The lack of a recognizable identity in Canada is a problem for immigrants. Newcomers want to integrate into their new country, but do not know how or what it is to be Canadian.

Multiculturalism does not help. Being told you can keep your culture can be irritating to people who have left or fled their culture. Official multiculturalism is also at odds with the unofficial views of many in Canada.

"There are too many immigrants coming into this country who are not adopting Canadian values."

A Focus Canada survey posed this question and 66%, a clear majority of Canadians agreed.

Even more, 76% wanted assimilation: *"Ethnic groups should try as much as possible to blend into Canadian society and not form a separate community."*[96]

Surveys almost always show a substantial difference between official Canadian positions, such as multiculturalism, and actual opinions of Canadians, such as assimilation. This supports the theory that Canada has an official false self in favour of high immigration and multiculturalism. While this country's true self is less interested in immigration, multiculturalism and refugees.

The question of assimilation for newcomers is what exactly is Canadian society? It is difficult if not impossible to integrate into a vacuum, or a society unsure of itself.

Canada has shared traditions and values and needs to be more confident and assertive of these.

The Focus Canada survey stated that "first and foremost Canadians identify their country as being free and democratic."

The solution to every problem

All the reasons why Canada needs immigration — and more of it

Perhaps immigration is Canada's identity. It seems to be everything else. Every problem in Canada can seemingly be solved with more immigrants.

The housing market is slowing. We need more immigrants. Not enough construction workers to build the houses, we need more immigrants. Not enough skilled workers, entrepreneurs, investors, farmers, health care workers and tech workers. We need more immigrants. Aging baby boomers need pension payers. Schools and universities need students. Small towns need residents. White people need culture. The growing national debt needs taxpayers. And so on.

Immigration in Canada is policy laziness. Our elected leaders only have one decision to make, how much more newcomers. To fix every problem, to solve every shortage. To pay every deficit. Who needs reform or new ideas when we have immigrants?

It's amazing that immigration can resolve all our troubles while causing no problems. There are of course no problems or costs with high levels of immigration. To suggest that would be racist.

Immigration is a blunt tool that gets the credit of a sharp specialized instrument. It is blunt because immigrants are people, unpredictable people with their own self interest, goals, and faults. They're not going to buy condos to 'support the market' when it is crashing, just because you want them to. They're not going to live in northern communities just because it makes the country more geographically balanced. Newcomers are assumed to be too naïve to avoid a crashing market or too desperate to do jobs Canadians don't want.

The non-immigrant population of Canada is also wronged by this panacea of immigration. Born Canadians are treated as a spent force, lethargic, unable to change to meet any new need. If they have the wrong skills or education, it's no big deal, just add immigrants.

In a 2018 Ontario election debate, now Premier, then candidate Doug Ford committed the cardinal sin of Canadian politics. On a question of bringing immigrants to fill jobs in northern Ontario, Ford was *supposed to* say 'diversity is our strength, more immigrants'.

But he didn't. For some strange reason, Doug Ford said we should "take care of our own first" and "exhaust every single avenue and we don't have anyone who can fulfill the job" before using schemes to pull newcomers to the north. Opponents called Ford's comments shocking, insulting, and worrisome.[97]

Outrageous, he suggested that employers should consider locals first, before looking for overseas workers. This is scandalous in a society where foreign immigration is the answer to every question. Training and employing born and naturalized Canadians, especially indigenous Canadians, should be the priority of Canadian governments. But that is too difficult and archaic.

Canadians want local lettuce and foreign labour. Most politicians will gladly oblige. Nothing can compete with our altar of immigration.

Numbers

A key question is how many newcomers per year. For 2019, Canada targeted 330,000, increasing to 350,000 for 2021. In October 2020, the government announced new immigration targets of 401,000 in 2021, 411,000 in 2022, and 421,000 in 2023. Of course, the new targets are higher and rising.[98]

In Canadian logic, the Covid-19 health crisis, worldwide pandemic, and economic recession resulted in a need for more immigrants, not less.

400,000 newcomers per year would be about 1% of Canada's population of 38 million.

NOVEMBER 6, 2018 3:10PM

Canada Will Up Immigration to 1% of its Population, 2.6 Times the U.S. Rate

BY DAVID J. BIER

Framed as '1% of the population', these numbers seem low. Deceptively low. We did not end up with 21% of Canada born overseas with low immigration. Canada is famed for its high intake of newcomers. Reporting *annual* immigration as a percentage of the total population is intended to portray a small number. What can be lower than 1%.

A more accurate way to look at immigration considers how long it takes newcomers to get settled. Immigrant

Services Association of Nova Scotia describes a four-stage adaptation to the new country. Euphoria, disenchantment, gradual adjustment, and acceptance. The disenchantment stage is the most notable. Feelings of frustration, disappointment, homesickness, and having no connection to Canada dominate this period.[99] It takes years to get your career going and learn the system.

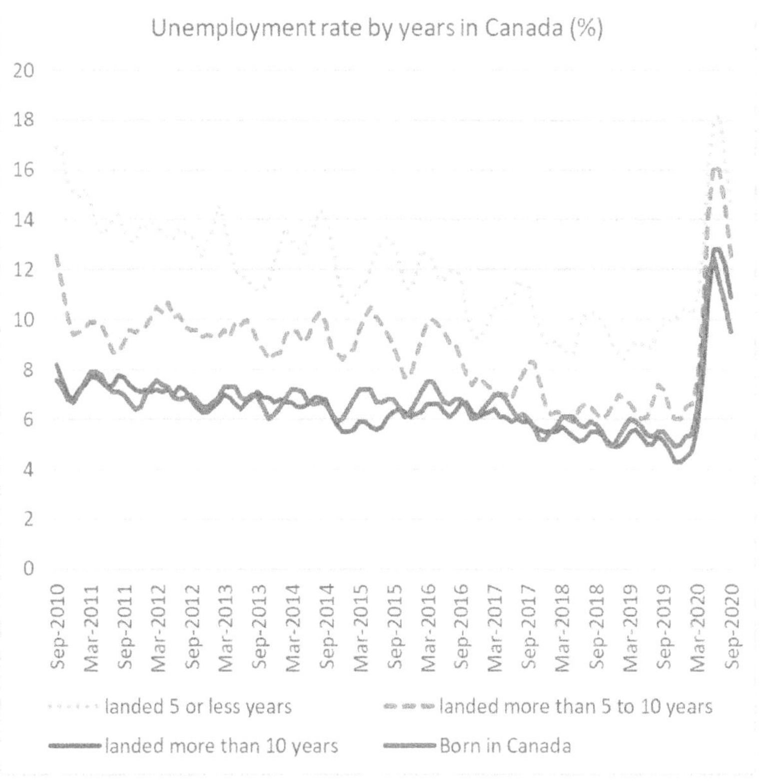

A graph of the unemployment rate shows it is significantly higher for immigrants landed 5 years or less. In the past decade this averaged 12% versus 6.5% for those in Canada more than 10 years.[100] (Note the large spike across all categories due to Covid-19).

The City of Toronto defines 'recent immigrants' as coming within 10 years.[101] Optimistically, Statistics Canada defines recent as within 5 years. Assuming it takes 5 years for a new immigrant to get settled, at any point in time, there's 5 years worth of migration not yet adapted to Canada. 5 years of 400,000 per year is 2,000,000 unintegrated newcomers. Two million newcomers, mostly crowded into a few cities, not sprinkled across the country.

Looking at immigration this way reveals the scale of the issue. A politically correct culture where Canadians are only allowed to praise immigration and not criticize also hides the problems of mass migration.

Immigration is unique among public policy. It is a policy that cannot be reversed. Taxes and regulations can be changed and undone. There is no undo button for migration. You cannot deport large numbers of people. Once immigrants are here, they are here permanently. Their values, culture, problems, hate, and all.

For immigration to succeed in Canada, fewer newcomers are needed. In 2006, a Toronto Star article stated that unless Canada reduces immigration, Toronto would not be able to maintain social and physical infrastructure.[102] This was back when Canada took 'only' about 250,000 newcomers per year.

2021's target is 400,000 people. Immigration is biased towards rising numbers for many reasons:

- Political correctness: immigration is officially good. You're not supposed to talk about negative aspects of immigration. Don't be racist.
- Corporate lobby: big businesses need more consumers and a steady source of new labour.
- Vote banks: Political parties now rely on immigrants as swing votes. A few immigrant heavy ridings can decide elections.

- Auction effect: The political party with the highest immigration target wins the 'most pro-immigrant contest'.

- State Multiculturalism: Canada is multicultural. Criticism of multiculturalism is therefore unpatriotic criticism of Canada.

- Validation: Immigration is Canada's drug habit that feeds our self-esteem. It's needed to validate ourselves as a progressive open country.

Canada needs a more mature immigration policy. The era of stroking our ego with immigrants is over. Auctioning ever higher numbers of newcomers is blind and mistaken. Newcomers are increasingly disappointed in the real Canada compared to the myth they were sold.

Recent analysis by Statistics Canada highlighted one problem of high immigration, over-education. There are too many university-educated immigrants and not enough jobs requiring that education. Statistics Canada never used the word *problem*, since you're not supposed to imply problems with too much immigration.

"Over-education has negative consequences for both individual workers and a country's economy."

"University-educated immigrants accounted for 70% of the growth in low-skilled employment."

"This study shows that the growth in employment requiring a university education from 2001 to 2016 lagged behind the rising supply of university-educated workers in Canada." The study also implied (very covertly) that educated newcomers compete in the labour market with Canadian born youth.[103] It carefully avoids any suggestion that high levels of immigration is problematic.

Concealing the issues of mass immigration and multiculturalism is accruing problems that will one day need to be solved.

News / Economy

Why Canada still needs immigrants despite soaring unemployment

Immigrants drive economic growth in Canada, and a slowdown brought on by the pandemic could have repercussions for decades

Gabriel Friedman

Jun 18, 2020 • Last Updated 5 months ago • 8 minute read

Coronavirus

Perhaps Canada is not mature enough to say no to large scale immigration. Maybe we are too concerned with being 'open' compared to a closed America. No Prime Minister wants to get their hands dirty cutting immigration.

The Covid-19 coronavirus shutdown of 2020 did the deed for us. Travel and migration have been severely curtailed around the world. Numbers have been cut, whether Canada wanted it or not. Maybe from this disaster we can re-evaluate our priorities and put more prudence into policymaking. No, it's not the Canadian way. The new and higher 400,000 per year targets announced in October 2020 is a prime example of always-higher-immigration policy.

Immigration Minister Marco Mendicino stated, "put simply, we need more workers, and immigration is the way to get there."[104] Right when the second wave of

Covid-19 is striking, and businesses are once again closing their doors. "We need more workers."

A major justification for high immigration has always been that the economy needed it. Covid-19 has shut down large sectors of the economy and some businesses will soon be bankrupt. Millions of Canadians were made unemployed during the pandemic recession. There's going to be more workers than jobs for the next few years. This should have been enough to say to the corporate lobby that fewer newcomers are needed.

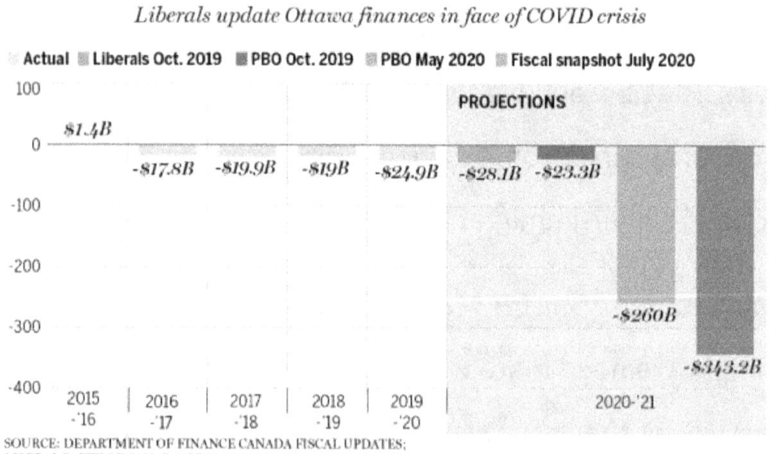

Another result of the covid-19 recession is massive deficits and debt. In the preceding good economic years, the federal government and some provinces (especially Ontario) spent well above their revenues. In theory governments should save or balance the budget during the good years. But this is Canada, a fairy land. Large deficits during the good years will now be followed by massive deficits during the Covid recession. Municipal governments will especially face a fiscal reckoning since they cannot borrow to fund operating deficits.

The coming austerity must also be applied to immigration. The costs of immigration that largely fall on cities need to take precedence over national boasting. *Immigration austerity*, that should sound better to a population concerned with nice-sounding labels.

Quiet hopes that Covid-19 era immigration would be left at lower levels were dashed with the 400,000 per year announcement. Pandemic? Recession? Immigration and citizenship backlog? No problem, full steam ahead. Increasing inflows in the face of unprecedented uncertainty is evidence of the arrogant nature of this immortal country.

Canada is not immortal

Many issues and problems are raised in this book. Unfortunately, they are not easily fixed. Some are inherent with any immigration system. Such as the question of how far to assimilate. However, there are problems caused by typical Canadian pretenses and our tolerance for nonsense. A bureaucratic legal system without regard for common sense. Excessive government funding for bourgeois amenities like the CBC. A cost of living needlessly high without empathy for the poor. Barriers to interprovincial trade that worsen our geographical separation.

Some problems are ideological, a politicized education system, doctrinaire health care, and ever encroaching political correctness. Cultural traits like politeness and complacency need to be viewed critically for the unseen costs they impose on society.

Pierre Trudeau once referred to Themistocles' realization that Athens was not immortal. "I think we have to realize that Canada is not immortal."[105] Canada is indeed not immortal, or perfect. Or inherently better than America or any other myth we have. We can lose Canada, as it degrades, living on only in past glory. The first step to solving our problems is to acknowledge them. This is a nation in progress that needs nation building. This book isn't meant to condemn Canada but to start the much-needed repairs. The second step is to consider why so many immigrants have come and want to come to Canada in the first place.

In Canada and elsewhere, freedom of speech is on the endangered list

July 4, 2019 By John Cooper

Freedom of speech. Freedom of the press. These phrases may conjure up Hollywood-style images of noble activists and principled reporters butting heads with those in power – and winning.

Atwood joins dozens of public figures in warning against threat to free speech

By Levon Sevunts |
english@rcinet.ca
Posted: Wednesday, July 8, 2020 11:39
Last Updated: Wednesday, July 8, 2020 11:42

Free speech in Canada: It was bad five years ago. Do you think it's gotten better since?

Barbara Kay examines 'cancel culture' on Canadian campuses as part of the National Post's 'Free speech in Canada' series

Barbara Kay
Nov 13, 2019 • Last Updated 11 months ago • 5 minute read

Why We Migrate

It is often taken for granted why newcomers come to Canada. Most assume because Canada is richer and better than other countries. But this isn't 1986 anymore. It is not clear that Canada is still a richer country with more opportunity.

Opportunity is often used as a catch-all reason for coming to Canada. But newcomers do not come to Canada simply for financial benefit. Any analysis of the costs of immigration, and the cost of living in Canada should make this clear. There is more business in China, more wealth in Saudi Arabia, more diversity in India and more culture in Brazil. There is more money to be made and no taxes to be paid in the Arabian Gulf. Why the booming international middle class should leave their homes and come to Canada is no longer obvious.

This may be difficult for Canadians to understand, but immigrants are not necessarily eager for Canada in particular, but the Western world in general and the

Anglosphere in particular. We forget that before Canada was the international land of opportunity, America was. Foreigners are as eager to go to the US, England, Australia and New Zealand.

It is sometimes alleged that some immigrants are incompatible with Western values in countries like Canada. It is more often forgotten that immigrants come to Canada *because* of its Western values.

Western values are the only amenities that cannot be purchased in Dubai, Beijing or Jakarta. Regardless of how rich you are. No amount of armed guards and servants will make you as safe and comfortable as an implemented Charter of Rights and Freedoms.

Individual rights, gender equality, merit, the rule of law, innocent until proven guilty. These values are usually taken for granted and sometimes actively opposed. It is now fashionable to romanticize other cultures and civilizations while demonizing Western civilization. Try explaining this to immigrants who couldn't wait to leave those other cultures and migrate to the evil, racist, imperialist Western world.

The values and rights established and applied in the West are the main attraction for immigrants. And a source of pride for Canadians as the Focus Canada poll showed. "First and foremost, Canadians identify their country as being free and democratic". Democratic freedoms are the traits mutually desired by newcomers and born Canadians alike. The common denominator needed to build and reinforce Canada.

Unfortunately, across North America, individual rights and freedoms are under threat. Freedom of speech in particular, which is being curtailed to avoid causing offence.

As Tom Kott wrote in the Huffington Post: "This societal need to prosecute potty mouths and anything deemed offensive has become a popular trend in Canada."[106]

With the covid-19 virus shutdown, many public freedoms were suppressed, understandably to control the pandemic. Canadians locked themselves indoors, less free than accustomed to. Our freedoms that remain must be prized and protected. Especially the ones pledged by our Charter.

As the federal Department of Justice explains "We're free to think our own thoughts, speak our minds, listen to views of others and express our opinions in creative ways."[107]

In a nation beset by political correctness, politeness, and conformity, we are still constitutionally guaranteed "freedom of thought, belief, opinion and expression, including freedom of the press and other media of communication."

Our rights and freedoms are "subject only to such reasonable limits prescribed by law as can be demonstrably justified in a free and democratic society."

It's important to emphasize that those reasonable limits on our freedom should be demonstrably justified in a free and democratic society. The norm is freedom, limits are the exception. It is the Charter of Rights and

Freedoms. Not the Charter of Conformity and

Restrictions, where freedoms may be granted certain

permissions.

Whereas Canada is founded upon principles that recognize the supremacy of God and the rule of law:

Guarantee of Rights and Freedoms

1. The *Canadian Charter of Rights and Freedoms* guarantees the rights and freedoms set out in it subject only to such reasonable limits prescribed by law as can be demonstrably justified in a free and democratic society.

Fundamental Freedoms

2. Everyone has the following fundamental freedoms: (*a*) freedom of conscience and religion; (*b*) freedom of thought, belief, opinion and expression, including freedom of the press and other media of communication; (*c*) freedom of peaceful assembly; and (*d*) freedom of association.

First section of the Canadian Charter of Rights and Freedoms

They Desire a Better Country

Desiderantes Meliorem Patriam. Latin for *Desiring a Better Country*. It's inscribed on the Coat of Arms and Order of Canada medals. From the Bible, it refers to Abraham and his family leaving their home looking for a better country, directed by God.

Abraham was told to find a better land, not in materials terms. But a 'heavenly' country, better in values.

Ultimately, Canada cannot compete with the material wealth of the Emirates, or the warmer climate of tropical lands. Our comparative advantage is in our values, and respect for individual rights and freedoms.

Fundamental values and freedoms matter more than the cost of living or other policies. It is the basis for everything else in society. This is why the Charter emphasizes democratic individual rights. A free society will be more entrepreneurial, artistic, inventive and prosperous in the long term.

Trade offs will appear, such as protecting collective secularism in Quebec versus individual freedom of religion. The individual's rights should take precedence. A person's right to self-preservation (health care) is more important than the national desire to feel egalitarian. Politeness and conformity are not good enough reasons to suppress free speech.

Canada prides itself in being 'open' collectively but not individually. Individual freedoms are necessary for the success of immigration, especially freedom of speech and thought. Problems with migration and culture are piling up under a stifling rug of over-sensitivity. Canadians are self censoring, afraid to discuss issues, fearing accusations of racism or xenophobia. Criticizing anything related to immigration is sacrilege. Problems don't get solved or even discussed because of political correctness. Festering until they boil over. Canadians will sneer at America's hate of immigrants until they realize it's only a few years away in Canada. Candidly and freely discussing migration is the only way to preserve it.

This book is not meant to start a conversation about immigration. Conversations about immigration are already happening, praise in public and criticism in private. This is a call to save our ability to have conversations about complex topics in a public democratic way. Our constitutional freedom of opinion *and expression,* without vicious accusations of blasphemy. Violent mobs claiming offence is why we left Pakistan. Shutting down of dissent is why we left Russia. Facing punishment for writing wrong opinions is why we left Iran. Losing your job because of your beliefs is why we left China.

Canada comes close to having a second world and third world mentality. Prioritizing collective rights of groups, national myths, political control of the population, and 'standing up to America' are habits common in worse countries. Many immigrants come to Canada expecting better, only to see the same problems we left behind. Democracy mostly in theory, corruption, elitist leadership, controlled media, politicized institutions, and the fear of an offended mob.

Canada has the inheritance of a first world democracy but the tendencies of a small country. We have built a great nation, but one unsure of itself. Our building blocks must be remembered and reinforced, from the fundamental rights of individuals to economic freedom.

Separatism and alienation will come with our geography but can be mitigated with common values.

Immigrants must want to come to Canada based on our reality not our marketing. And if that reality is less than perfect, then let us learn to be proud of an imperfect country.

Most importantly immigration must be treated as a national policy, not a national religion. A policy that can be discussed democratically and respectfully. Where dissidents aren't demonized, accused of racism and shunned into silence. If Canadians are not free to think, believe and express themselves, then Canada will not be worth coming to.

About the Author

Joel Binda came to Canada in 1997 at 11 years old. From a small village in southern Trinidad & Tobago, with a Trinidadian mother and Guyanese father. Coming to Canada permanently on a *Visitor's Visa* shows the cloudy sphere that is immigration.

He studied finance at Ryerson University in Toronto and worked in both public sector finance and banking.

Inequalities, especially economic inequality, led to his interest in economics, history, and politics.

Joel lived mostly in immigrant dense communities in Mississauga and Toronto, Ontario. In 2007, Joel became a Canadian citizen. Noticing a persistent difference in what immigrants expressed amongst themselves versus what was publicly spoken, this book was born.

With 21st century politics and literature becoming ever more censored and politically correct. *What Immigrants Hate about Canada* had to be written. It couldn't wait any longer. In a couple of years, it may be forbidden to write certain things. Or Canadian immigration might be broken beyond repair under the weight of naivety and pretense.

Nevertheless, Joel still thinks of himself as a finance guy instead of a writer. As William Saroyan wrote, "a man must pretend not to be a writer."

For requests or other contact, write to the email address: differentcanada@gmail.com

Note on Sources

The sources for this book have been mainstream news, magazines and surveys. CBC News, Toronto Star, Globe and Mail, National Post. Even articles from the Huffington Post Canada. Surveys were from professional polling firms such as Abacus, Angus Reid, Environics. Government websites were also cited.

Care was taken to avoid extremist or radical sources, although they can be easily found. Mainstream sources were used for two reasons. Firstly, to demonstrate that opinions in this book are not extreme. Secondly, to show that issues discussed here are openly available but often ignored.

Endnotes by Chapter

HATE:

[1] Population by generation status and median age. 2016 Census of Population. *Statistics Canada.*
https://www12.statcan.gc.ca/census-recensement/2016/as-sa/fogs-spg/Facts-can-eng.cfm?Lang=Eng&GK=CAN&GC=01&TOPIC=7

DISLOYAL:

[2] Canadian flags ordered down: Williams. (2004). *CBC News.*
https://www.cbc.ca/news/canada/newfoundland-labrador/canadian-flags-ordered-down-williams-1.505946

[3] Gall, G. (2013). Quebec Referendum (1995). *The Canadian Encyclopedia.*
https://www.thecanadianencyclopedia.ca/en/article/quebec-referendum-1995

[4] Perspectives on independence in Alberta. (May 2020). *Western Standard.*
https://www.westernstandardonline.com/wp-content/uploads/2020/05/Western-Standard-Research-May-25th.pdf

[5] O'Toole, E. (2014). I want to be Canadian – but why should I have to swear allegiance to the Queen? *The Guardian.*
https://www.theguardian.com/commentisfree/2014/aug/14/canadian-swear-allegiance-queen-oath-hereditary

[6]   In Wake of Constitutional Crisis, New Survey Demonstrates that Canadians Lack Basic Understanding of our Country's Parliamentary System. (2008). *Ipsos.* https://www.ipsos.com/en-ca/wake-constitutional-crisis-new-survey-demonstrates-canadians-lack-basic-understanding-our-countrys

DISCONTENT:

[7]   Hui, S. (2010). Vancouver protesters burn Canadian flag during march in solidarity with G20 detainees, black bloc. *Georgia Straight.* https://www.straight.com/article-332171/vancouver/vancouver-g20-protesters-burn-canadian-flag-march-solidarity-detainees-black-bloc

KANADA:

[8]   Warnica, R. (2019). Hong Kong student living in Toronto strikes a nerve on Twitter with eerie observations about Canadian life. *National Post. (*Shoji Ushiyama) https://nationalpost.com/news/canada/hong-kong-student-living-in-toronto-strikes-a-nerve-on-twitter-with-eerie-observations-about-canadian-life

LE BOURGEOIS ÉMIGRÉ:

[9]   Hou, F., Lu, Y., Schimmele, C. (2019). Recent Trends in Over-education by Immigration Status. *Statistics Canada.* https://www150.statcan.gc.ca/n1/pub/11f0019m/11f0019m2019024-eng.htm

[10]   Proof of funds – Skilled immigrants (Express Entry).
Immigration, Refugees and Citizenship Canada. Government of
Canada.
https://www.canada.ca/en/immigration-refugees-
citizenship/services/immigrate-canada/express-
entry/documents/proof-funds.html

POOR IMMIGRANTS:
[11]   Lamman, C., MacIntyre, H., Hunt, D., (2017). Minimum wage
hikes will hurt young people, immigrants. *Fraser Institute.*
https://www.fraserinstitute.org/article/minimum-wage-hikes-
will-hurt-young-people-immigrants?language=en

MIDDLE CLASS POLITICS:

[12]   Lum, Z. (2019). Asked To Define 'Middle Class,' Trudeau Says
'Canadians Know'. *HuffPost.*
https://www.huffingtonpost.ca/entry/justin-trudeau-middle-
class_ca_5df92734e4b03aed50f7085f

OTHER IMMIGRANTS:

[13]   Cohen, S., Roach, J., Charles, L. (2006). Borat: Cultural Learnings
of America for Make Benefit Glorious Nation of Kazakhstan.

[14]   Smith, H. (2005). Mein Kampf sales soar in Turkey. *The
Guardian.*
https://www.theguardian.com/world/2005/mar/29/turkey.bo
oks

[15]   Peters, R. (2006). Outsourced.

[16]   Hou, F., Lu, Y., Schimmele, C. (2019). Recent Trends in Over-education by Immigration Status. *Statistics Canada.* https://www150.statcan.gc.ca/n1/pub/11f0019m/11f0019m2019024-eng.htm

RACISM:

[17]   Amha, M. (2020). What Americans then to get wrong about racism in Canada. *Maclean's.* https://www.msn.com/en-ca/news/canada/what-americans-tend-to-get-wrong-about-racism-in-canada/ar-BB17nVLR

[18]   Mayor McCallion under fire for alleged anti-immigrant remarks. (2001). *CBC News.* https://www.cbc.ca/news/canada/mayor-mccallion-under-fire-for-alleged-anti-immigrant-remarks-1.281665

[19]   Ho, S. (2019). Don Cherry's history of controversial comments. *CTV News.* https://www.ctvnews.ca/sports/don-cherry-s-history-of-controversial-comments-1.4680505

MULTICULTURALISM:

[20]   Bissoondath, N. (1994). Selling Illusions: The Cult of Multiculturalism in Canada.

[21]   Reid, A. (2016). Canadians aren't as accepting as we think — and we can't ignore it, writes Angus Reid. *CBC News.* https://www.cbc.ca/news/canada/angus-reid-poll-canadian-values-immigration-1.3789223

FIRST NATIONS:

[22] Honouring the Truth, Reconciling for the Future. (2015). *Truth and Reconciliation Commission of Canada.* http://www.trc.ca/assets/pdf/Honouring_the_Truth_Reconciling_for_the_Future_July_23_2015.pdf

[23] Sowell, T. (1985). The Economics and Politics of Race: An International Perspective.

[24] The Oath of Citizenship. (2019). Immigration, Refugees and Citizenship Canada. https://www.canada.ca/en/immigration-refugees-citizenship/news/2019/05/the-oath-of-citizenship.html

BETTER-THAN-AMERICAN-STAN:

[25] Kwong, M. (2019). Trump wants an immigration system 'like they have in Canada.' Would a merit-based plan work in the U.S.? *CBC News.* https://www.cbc.ca/news/world/trump-immigration-system-canada-merit-based-points-1.5115475

[26] Frey, W. (2018). The US will become 'minority white' in 2045, Census projects. *Brookings.* https://www.brookings.edu/blog/the-avenue/2018/03/14/the-us-will-become-minority-white-in-2045-census-projects/

MUSLIMS:

[27] Muslims the Target of Most Racial Bias. (2016). Forum Research.

28   Bascaramurty, D., Alphonso C. (2017). A community divided. *The Globe and Mail.* https://www.theglobeandmail.com/news/toronto/a-community-divided-the-fight-over-canadian-values-threatens-to-boil-over-inpeel/article34852452/

29   Data leak reveals how China 'brainwashes' Uighurs in prison camps. (2019). *BBC News.* https://www.bbc.com/news/world-asia-china-50511063

30   Toronto 18: Key events in the case. (2008). *CBC News.* https://www.cbc.ca/news/canada/toronto-18-key-events-in-the-case-1.715266

31   Selley, C. (2015). Muslim community taking the lead in latest round of Ontario sex-education protests. *National Post.* https://nationalpost.com/news/canada/muslim-community-taking-the-lead-in-latest-round-of-ontario-sex-education-protests

32   Grenier E., (2016). Muslim Canadians increasingly proud of and attached to Canada, survey suggests. *CBC News.* https://www.cbc.ca/news/politics/grenier-muslim-canadians-environics-1.3551591

QUEBEC:

33   Tajik government issues hijab ban. (2005). *AlJazeera. https://www.aljazeera.com/news/2005/10/21/tajik-government-issues-hijab-ban*

34   Bilefsky D., (2020). A Quebec Ban on Religious Symbols Upends Lives and Careers. *The New York Times.*

https://www.nytimes.com/2020/03/07/world/canada/quebec-religious-symbols-ban.html

35   Nelles, M., Singh, M. (2016). New laws for Quebec signage. *Torys LLP.*
https://www.torys.com/insights/publications/2016/11/new-laws-for-quebec-signage

36   Woods, A. (2015). 'Money and ethnic votes': the words that shape Jacques Parizeau's legacy. *The Star.*
https://www.thestar.com/news/canada/2015/06/02/jacques-parizeau-former-quebec-premier-dead-at-84-spouse-says.html

37   Kingston A. (2012). Jan Wong dishes on depression in the workplace. *Maclean's.*
https://www.macleans.ca/culture/jan-wong-dishes-on-depression-in-the-workplace/

FREE HEALTH CARE:

38   Barua, B., Moir, M. (2020). Comparing Performance of Universal Health Care Countries, 2020. *Fraser Institute.*
https://www.fraserinstitute.org/studies/comparing-performance-of-universal-health-care-countries-2020

39   Day, B. (2010). In government we trust. *BC Medical Journal.*
https://bcmj.org/editorials/government-we-trust

40   Mason, G. (2018). B.C., where access to a wait-list is considered access to health care. *The Globe and Mail.*
https://www.theglobeandmail.com/opinion/article-bc-where-access-to-a-wait-list-is-considered-access-to-health-care/

41   Medical inadmissibility. Immigration, Refugees and Citizenship
      Canada.
      https://www.canada.ca/en/immigration-refugees-
      citizenship/services/immigrate-
      canada/inadmissibility/reasons/medical-inadmissibility.html

EDUCATION:

42   Children with an immigrant background: Bridging cultures.
      (2017). *Statistics Canada*.
      https://www12.statcan.gc.ca/census-recensement/2016/as-
      sa/98-200-x/2016015/98-200-x2016015-eng.cfm

43   The TDSB Grade 9 Cohort 2006-2011: TREND DATA Fact Sheet
      No. 1. Toronto District School Board.
      https://www.tdsb.on.ca/Portals/0/Community/Community%20
      Advisory%20committees/ICAC/research/September%202012%
      20Cohort%20dataAcrobat%20Document.pdf

44   Rankin, J., Rushowy K., Brown, L. (2013). Toronto school
      suspension rates highest for black and aboriginal students.
      Toronto Star.
      https://www.thestar.com/news/gta/2013/03/22/toronto_scho
      ol_suspension_rates_highest_for_black_and_aboriginal_stude
      nts.html

HIGHER EDUCATION:

45   Findlay, S., Kohler, N. (2010). The enrollment controversy*.
      Maclean's.
      https://www.macleans.ca/news/canada/too-asian/

46   McMarthy-Miller, B., (2020). "The Canadians of Africa". *Bob Hearts Abishola*. CBS.

INTERNATIONAL STUDENTS:

47   Canadian and international tuition fees by level of study, 2019/2020. Statistics Canada. https://www150.statcan.gc.ca/t1/tbl1/en/tv.action?pid=37100 04501

48   Todd, D. (2019). Female foreign students endure harassment, exploitation. *Vancouver Sun*. https://vancouversun.com/opinion/columnists/douglas-todd-female-foreign-students-endure-harassment-exploitation

49   Tomlinson, K. (2019). How an immigration scheme steers newcomers into Canadian trucking jobs – and puts lives at risk. *The Globe and Mail*. https://www.theglobeandmail.com/canada/article-foreign-truck-drivers-canada-immigration-investigation/

POLITICAL CORRECTNESS:

50   Mallick, H. (2020). Why we shouldn't call women 'menstruators'. *The Star*. https://www.thestar.com/politics/political-opinion/2020/06/12/when-we-change-language-to-help-some-we-should-be-careful-not-to-hurt-others.html

INDENTURED IMMIGRATION:

51   Mojtehedzadeh, S. (2017). This sexually abused migrant worker is now safe — but she knows others aren't. *The Star*.

https://www.thestar.com/news/canada/migrants/2017/10/07/
this-sexually-abused-migrant-worker-is-now-safe-but-she-
knows-others-arent.html

TELEVISION AND MEDIA:

[52]   CBC president compares Netflix influence to colonialism.
(2019). *CBC News.*
https://www.cbc.ca/news/entertainment/tait-netflix-
colonialism-analogy-1.5000657

[53]   "One man's guide to Canadian culture for Syrian refugees."
(2016). *This hour has 22 minutes.* CBC.
https://www.cbc.ca/22minutes/videos/clips-season-23/one-
mans-guide-to-canadian-culture-for-syrian-refugees

[54]   Focus Canada 2010, Public opinion research on the record.
Environics Institute.

[55]   2018-2019 Annual Report. CBC.
https://cbc.radio-canada.ca/en/impact-and-
accountability/finances/annual-reports/ar-2018-
2019/highlights/financial-highlights

[56]   Watson, W. (2019). William Watson: CBC's The National brings
Canadians all the news that's woke. *Financial Post.*
https://financialpost.com/opinion/william-watson-cbcs-the-
national-brings-canadians-all-the-news-thats-woke

[57]   Parry, T. (2019). Journalists question Liberal government's
$600M media bailout plan. *CBC News.*
https://www.cbc.ca/news/politics/journalists-question-media-
bailout-1.5147761

COST OF LIVING:

[58]   Harris, S. (2018). Canadians pay some of the highest wireless prices in the world — but report says they're worth it. *CBC News*. https://www.cbc.ca/news/business/wireless-prices-cell-phone-plan-canada-1.4652550#:~:text=Australia%20offers%20cheaper%20plans,to%20%2437%20less%20a%20month.

[59]   Crawley, M. (2017). Ontarians pay highest rates in Canada for hydro, study shows. *CBC News*. https://www.cbc.ca/news/canada/toronto/ontario-hydro-fraser-institute-study-1.4212668

OBEDIENT COMPLACENCY:

[60]   Ignatieff, M. (2004). Peace, Order and Good Government: A Foreign Policy Agenda for Canada

[61]   Cohen, A. (2017). Cohen: Captains of complacency – What if Canada is wasted on Canadians? *Ottawa Citizen.* https://ottawacitizen.com/opinion/columnists/cohen-captains-of-complacency-what-if-canada-is-wasted-on-canadians

SMUG LIFE:

[62]   Savage, L. (2017). Accounting for Histories: 150 Years of Canadian Maple Washing. *Open Canada*. https://opencanada.org/accounting-histories-150-years-canadian-maple-washing/

[63] McCullough, J. (2020). Canada's covid-19 second wave is a humbling moment after a summer of bragging. *The Washington Post.* https://www.washingtonpost.com/opinions/2020/11/30/canadas-covid-19-second-wave-is-humbling-moment-after-summer-bragging/

CHOICE SUPPORTIVE BIAS:

[64] Choice-Supportive Bias. *Conversion Uplift.* https://www.conversion-uplift.co.uk/glossary-of-conversion-marketing/choice-supportive-bias/

ASSIMILATION:

[65] Saroyan, W. (1934). Seventy Thousand Assyrians. Story Magazine & Literature Journal

[66] Sinikian, S. (2010). When genocide turns into suicide. *Armenian Youth Federation Western US.* https://ayfwest.org/news/when-genocide-turns-into-suicide/

[67] Serebrin, J. (2020). Armenian diaspora in Canada says Ottawa must act to prevent a second genocide. *The Globe and Mail.* https://www.theglobeandmail.com/canada/article-armenian-diaspora-in-canada-says-ottawa-must-act-to-prevent-a-second-2/

SMALL TOWN CANADA:

[68] Lajoie, E. (2020). Small Towns Are Dying. Can Immigration Save Them? *The Walrus.*

https://thewalrus.ca/small-towns-are-dying-can-immigration-save-them/

GEOGRAPHY:

[69] Gilmore, S. (2019). Canada: a nation of strangers. *Maclean's.* https://www.macleans.ca/opinion/canada-a-nation-of-strangers/#:~:text=Scott%20Gilmore%3A%20Canadians%20don%27t,We%20vacation%20elsewhere.&text=Every%20region%2C%20every%20province%2C%20sits%20in%20isolation.

CENTURY INITIATIVE:

[70] Century Initiative. https://www.centuryinitiative.ca/

CANADA IS BACK:

[71] 'We're back,' Justin Trudeau says in message to Canada's allies abroad. (2015). *National Post.* https://nationalpost.com/news/politics/were-back-justin-trudeau-says-in-message-to-canadas-allies-abroad

[72] Kasoff, M., James, P. (2013). Canadian Studies in the New Millennium, Second Edition. University of Toronto Press.

[73] Trudeau under fire for expressing admiration for China's 'basic dictatorship'. (2013). *CTV News.* https://www.ctvnews.ca/politics/trudeau-under-fire-for-expressing-admiration-for-china-s-basic-dictatorship-1.1535116

[74] Coletto, D. (2018). The Path to 2019: Women and the Liberal Vote. Abacus Data.

https://abacusdata.ca/womenandtheliberalvote/

DEFICITS AND DEBT:

75 Mahboubi, P. (2019). Intergenerational Fairness: Will Our Kids Live Better than We Do? *C.D. Howe Institute.* https://www.cdhowe.org/sites/default/files/attachments/rese arch_papers/mixed/Commentary%20529%20English.pdf

76 Lovely, W., Schleich, T., Paquet, J. (Oct 14, 2020). Canada Watch. *National Bank of Canada.* https://www.nbc.ca/content/dam/bnc/en/rates-and-analysis/economic-analysis/hot-charts-201014.pdf

FOREIGN AID:

77 Statistical report on international assistance 2018-2019. Global Affairs Canada. https://www.international.gc.ca/gac-amc/publications/odaaa-lrmado/sria-rsai-2018-19.aspx?lang=eng

FOREIGN POLICY:

78 Simmons, T. (2019). A 'watershed' moment: How the 2009 Gardiner shutdown inspired a generation of Tamil leaders. *CBC News.* https://www.cbc.ca/news/canada/toronto/a-watershed-moment-how-the-2009-gardiner-shutdown-inspired-a-generation-of-tamil-leaders-1.5130342

79 Armenian diaspora in Canada says Ottawa must act to prevent a second genocide. (2020). *CP24, The Canadian Press.* https://www.cp24.com/news/armenian-diaspora-in-canada-

says-ottawa-must-act-to-prevent-a-second-genocide-
1.5142250

REFUGEES:

80   Immigration and Multiculturalism. (2010) Focus Canada.
Environics Institute.
https://www.environicsinstitute.org/docs/default-
source/project-documents/focus-canada-2010/immigration-
and-multiculturalism.pdf?sfvrsn=678ae6d1_2

81   Two-thirds call irregular border crossings a 'crisis,' more trust
Scheer to handle issue than Trudeau. (2018). *Angus Reid
Institute.*
http://angusreid.org/safe-third-country-asylum-seekers/

82   Immigration: Half back current targets, but colossal
misperceptions, pushback over refugees, cloud debate. (2019).
Angus Reid Institute.
http://angusreid.org/election-2019-immigration/

CONSULTANTS:

83   Starting again: improving government oversight of immigration
consultants. (2017). Report of the standing committee on
citizenship and immigration. House of Commons Report.
https://www.ourcommons.ca/DocumentViewer/en/42-
1/CIMM/report-11/page-66

84   Smith, MD. (2018). Trudeau tweet caused influx of refugee
inquiries, confusion within government, emails reveal. *National
Post.*
https://nationalpost.com/news/politics/trudeau-tweet-caused-

influx-of-refugee-inquiries-confusion-within-government-emails-reveal

85   Irregular border crosser statistics. Immigration and Refugee Board of Canada. https://irb-cisr.gc.ca/en/statistics/Pages/Irregular-border-crosser-statistics.aspx

LEGAL SYSTEM:

86   Rush, C., Yang, J. (2010). Grocer not guilty in citizen's arrest case. *The Star.* https://www.thestar.com/news/gta/2010/10/29/grocer_not_guilty_in_citizens_arrest_case.html

87   Starr, K., Kapelos, V. (2018). More than 20 child killers sent to healing lodges since 2011, figures show. *CBC News.* https://www.cbc.ca/news/politics/child-killers-transferred-healing-lodges-1.4903540

88   Public Perception of Crime and Justice in Canada: A Review of Opinion Polls. Department of Justice, Canada. https://www.justice.gc.ca/eng/rp-pr/csj-sjc/crime/rr01_1/p2_1.html#section2

89   Confidence in the justice system: Visible minorities have less faith in courts than other Canadians. (2018). Angus Reid Institute. http://angusreid.org/justice-system-confidence/#:~:text=In%20the%202016%20edition%20of,police%20force%20or%20RCMP%20detachment.

90   Klippenstein, M. (2018). Open letter to the treasurer and benchers of the law society. *StopSOP*. http://stopsop.ca/resources/your-letters-to-the-law-society/open-letter-to-the-treasurer-and-benchers-of-the-law-society/

91   Rong, T. (2019). The Law Society Should Not Get to Decide My Principles. *Ultravires*. http://ultravires.ca/2019/06/the-law-society-should-not-get-to-decide-my-principles/

POLITENESS:

92   McLaren, L. (2002). Canadian Martel wins Booker. *The Globe and Mail*. https://www.theglobeandmail.com/life/canadian-martel-wins-booker/article757348/

THE UNICORN AND THE UNICORN:

93   Lowen, Alexander. (1984). Narcissism: Denial of the true self. Simon & Schuster.

IDENTITY:

94   Gimblett, R. Dissension in the ranks: the 'mutinies' that never were. Royal Canadian Navy History. *Government of Canada*. https://www.canada.ca/en/navy/services/history/dissension-in-the-ranks.html

95   Lawson, G. (2015). Trudeau's Canada, Again. *The New York Times Magazine*. https://www.nytimes.com/2015/12/13/magazine/trudeaus-

canada-again.html

[96] Focus Canada 2010, Public opinion research on the record. Environics Institute.

THE SOLUTION TO EVERY PROBLEM:

[97] Walsh, M. (2018). 'I'm taking care of our own first,' Ford says on immigration. *iPolitics*. https://ipolitics.ca/2018/05/11/im-taking-care-of-our-own-first-ford-says-on-immigration/

NUMBERS:

[98] Harris, K. (2020). Federal government plans to bring in more than 1.2M immigrants in next 3 years. *CBC News*. https://www.cbc.ca/news/politics/mendicino-immigration-pandemic-refugees-1.5782642

[99] Stages of adapting to life in Canada. *Immigrant Services Association of Nova Scotia*. https://www.isans.ca/get-settled/community-wellness-services/stages-of-adapting-to-life-in-canada/

[100] Statistics Canada. Table 14-10-0082-01 Labour force characteristics by immigrant status, three-month moving average, unadjusted for seasonality https://www150.statcan.gc.ca/t1/tbl1/en/tv.action?pid=1410008201&pickMembers%5B0%5D=1.1&pickMembers%5B1%5D=3.8&pickMembers%5B2%5D=4.1&cubeTimeFrame.startMonth=09&cubeTimeFrame.startYear=2010&cubeTimeFrame.endMonth=09&cubeTimeFrame.endYear=2020&referencePeriods=20100901%2C20200901

[101] Toronto Newcomer Strategy. City of Toronto.

[102] Stoffman, D. (2006). When immigration goes awry. *Toronto Star.*
http://www.yorku.ca/goldring/clippings/immigration_awry.pdf

[103] Hou, F., Lu, Y., Schimmele, C. (2019). Recent Trends in Over-education by Immigration Status. *Statistics Canada.*
https://www150.statcan.gc.ca/n1/pub/11f0019m/11f0019m2019024-eng.htm

CORONAVIRUS:

[104] Harris, K. (2020). Federal government plans to bring in more than 1.2M immigrants in next 3 years. *CBC News.*
https://www.cbc.ca/news/politics/mendicino-immigration-pandemic-refugees-1.5782642

CANADA IS NOT IMMORTAL:

[105] Metcalf, K. (2016). Remembering Pierre: Justin Trudeau and the legacy of his father's charter. Canadian Journalists for Free Expression.
https://www.cjfe.org/remembering_pierre

WHY WE MIGRATE:

[106] Kott, T. (2016). Think Canada allows freedom of speech? Think again. *HuffPost.*
https://www.huffingtonpost.ca/tom-kott/freedom-of-speech-canada_b_2324999.html

[107] The rights and freedoms the Charter protects. Department of Justice. Canada.
https://www.justice.gc.ca/eng/csj-sjc/rfc-dlc/ccrf-ccdl/rfcp-cdlp.html